Created in Our Own Images.com
Fred M. Sander, M.D. (Editor)

Pygmalion and Galatea (1876)
by W.S. Gilbert

Introduction to the Art, Ethics, and Science of Cloning

Essays by Tom Freudenheim,
Jamie Love, Bill McKibben,
Lee M. Silver, Jonathan Shaw,
and Carolyn Williams

In conjunction with the centenary of
The New York Psychoanalytic Institute
1911–2011
www.psychoanalysis.org

IPBOOKS.net
International Psychoanalytic Books

A Division of International Psychoanalytic Media Group

ISBN: 978-0-615-39004-8

For our children and grandchildren,
who already know so much
in this new world:
Ari, Benjamin, Elizabeth,
Margot, Max, another Max,
Nina, Simon, Sophie and Susanna,
and all the generations to follow.

frontispiece

FREUD'S VIEW OF NARCISSISTIC LOVE

A person may love:—

(1) According to the narcissistic type:
    (a) what he himself is (i.e., himself),
    (b) what he himself was,
    (c) what he himself would like to be,
    [later elaborated as the person's ego ideal (p.101)]
    someone who was once a part of himself.

> —*Freud, S.* (1914) On Narcissism.
> *Standard Edition* Vol. XIV, p. 90.

In the interpersonal world this translates into someone loving, treating, or "sculpting" the other in the image(s) he has of the other or what I have called the Pygmalion-Galatea Process which emphasizes the reciprocal nature of relating or "sculpting" one another.

> —*Sander, F.M.* (2004) Psychoanalytic Couple Therapy.
> *Psychoanalytic Inquiry.* Vol. 24 #3, pp. 373–386.

Sculpting the other in the image of the other's ego ideal has recently been called *The Michelangelo Phenomenon.*

> —*Rusbult, CE, Finkel, E.J., & Kumashiro, M.* (2009).
> The Michelangelo Phenomenon.
> *Current Directions In Psychological Science*
> Vol. 18, #6. pp. 305–309.

CONTENTS

CONTRIBUTORS

Tom Freudenheim, Art historian and retired museum director (Baltimore, Worcester, Berlin, London). Most recently he served as Assistant Secretary for Museums at the Smithsonian. He writes regularly for the *Wall Street Journal* and other publications.

Jamie Love, Ph.D. Creator of internet series *Science Explained* at: http://www.synapses.co.uk/genetics/gene.html

Bill McKibben, Resident Scholar at Middlebury College. Author of *Eaarth: Making a Life on a Tough New Planet* (2010) by Times Books/Henry Holt and Founder of 350.org

Fred M. Sander, M.D. Associate Clinical Professor of Psychiatry, Weill-Cornell Medical School. Faculty, New York Psychoanalytic Institute and Society. Author, *Individual and Family Therapy: Toward an Integration.*(1979) Northvale, NJ: Jason Aronson.

Jonathan Shaw, Managing Editor, *Harvard Magazine.*

Lee M. Silver, Ph.D. Professor of Molecular Biology and Ethics, Princeton University. Author, *Challenging Nature: The Clash of Science at the Frontiers of Life* (2006) Ecco/Harper-Collins.

Carolyn Williams, Ph.D. Chair, Department of English, Rutgers University. Her book, *Gilbert and Sullivan: Gender, Genre, Parody,* is forthcoming from Columbia University Press in 2011.

Introduction
The Age of the Genome
Fred M. Sander, M.D.

> The times they are a changin'
> —*Bob Dylan (1964)*

This book is written for those of you who are coming of age in the 21st century, also known as Generation Y, the Millennial Generation. Or is it the iGeneration, as in iPhone, iPod and iPad? Or the Twitter Generation? As the speed of technology undoubtedly increases, future generations will no longer be known by phrases such as baby-boomers and post baby-boomers. Each new "generation" may have its own icon or image reflecting the latest innovation, for example, the "age of the internet," or one day, the "age of virtual reality." Whatever will signify your generation, most of you will be living much of your lives in the "age of the genome." I should include Generation X as well. The first baby born via in vitro fertilization in 1978, Louise Brown, today in her thirties, is a Generation X member. As these generations actually overlap, this book is for all who wish to be more informed about the rapidly changing world we share.

The rate of change in the past century—or the past millennium, as suggested in the cartoon below (Y1K)—will only speed up. While I

"WHAT ARE WE GOING TO DO ABOUT THE Y1K PROBLEM?"

have no crystal ball, this book is meant to help you grapple with the continued evolution of cultural changes and scientific advances. The contributors to this volume have tried to avoid technical language. We hope you see it as a form of continuing education. Some of you may want to immerse yourselves in the complex details of a discipline presented in this book or even pursue a career in that discipline. You may then gain some understanding to help bring about changes that could benefit, or possibly control threats to, our species and planet.

In my own childhood I remember sending cereal boxtops for any number of prizes, for example, a weather forecasting ring whose changing colors predicted rain or shine. I waited eagerly for a month until the ring arrived. Today my laptop, as does yours, informs me each day (or sometimes all day), "Welcome, you have mail" and provides new findings that our planet is, or is not, heating up. Television in the 1950s brought the first live baseball games with images of heroes not yet taking medications to improve their batting averages. In future generations, as you will read in Lee M. Silver's and Bill McKibben's chapters, athletes may one day be genetically endowed, for better or worse, with enhanced athletic skills by having had their genes manipulated before birth. On the larger world stage, will world leaders promote such biogenetic engineering for the treatment of cancer—or possibly for bio-terrorism?

When you begin to think of conceiving and raising your own children in this century of the genome, will you approve of genetic engineering, if available, to increase the athletic or intellectual prowess of your children? Will you approve the use of human embryos for the collection of stem cells to fight illnesses unamenable to current treatments? Will you seek genomic information in personal ads when seeking a partner to marry? In 1935 my uncles placed an ad in a newspaper to find a mate for their youngest sister. This is how my parents, living in small towns miles apart, met one another and later conceived me—clearly without assisted reproductive technology (ART).

Those of us who have lived most of our lives in the 20th century have experienced stormy times and moral quandaries not so different from those ahead of us. Revolutionary discoveries and changes in our understanding of the human mind, the atom, and of the universe we live in have brought remarkable advances. Freud left his imprint on our culture with his delineation of how our unconscious wishes rule so much of our lives. One of his insights, our tendency to be self-destructive, should serve as a warning that we humans have a tendency to turn our new discoveries against ourselves.

The many giants in post-Newtonian quantum physics (such as Einstein, Bohr, Fermi, Szilard, Heisenberg, and many others) made discoveries that led to the understanding of atomic physics, making possible nuclear weapons as well as nuclear medicine. Scientists have also extended the life span for those fortunate enough to benefit from advances in modern medicine and public health. At the current rate of change, half of you in the millennial generation will reach the age of one hundred and enter the 22nd century, absent unforeseen political upheavals or environmental catastrophes. One of these, the active oil spill in the Gulf of Mexico, continued unabated as I wrote (7/10/10) this introduction. Extended life spans, however, without increasing health in our post golden years would be a mixed blessing.

The recent sequencing of the genome will surely influence both our genetic and cultural inheritances. Though providing few new answers, this book will help to create greater awareness of these rapidly unfolding discoveries and may allow us to exert more enlightened control over a new "brave new world."

In order to achieve the aim of this book I have invited a number of scholars and professionals in both the humanities and sciences to respond to questions raised by a previously forgotten nineteenth century play, *Pygmalion and Galatea*, written by W.S. Gilbert (1876). I have rediscovered, revived, and here republished this play (slightly altered) to illustrate how cultural myths evolve and reflect the times in which they were created. The myth of Pygmalion, one of our creation myths, expresses the wish to create others in the images we would like them to be. The Roman poet Ovid (2004), in the 1st century, recorded this myth about a sculptor, Pygmalion, who creates a statue in his image of a perfect woman with whom he falls in love.

I chose this play because it sheds light on constancies in human nature: for example, the wishes to create, and be created, along with the attendant anxieties related to inborn sexual and aggressive wishes of early childhood. These universal human characteristics occur in ever-changing social circumstances. Gilbert's adaptation of the Pygmalion myth, written in the context of Victorian England, underscores that era's insistence on exclusive monogamy and the sinfulness of infidelity. There is no shortage of adaptations of the Pygmalion myth in 19th century literature (Joshua, 2001). Why did I pick this forgotten though once very popular play? Gilbert's drama not only anticipates psychoanalysis in the 20th century, but also, written a hundred years before the discovery of stem cells, it metaphorically resonates with the 21st century of genomic medicine. In Gilbert's play, written eighteen centuries after Ovid, Pygmalion creates many copies (i.e., clones) of his wife, Cynisca. One of these copies, Galatea, spontaneously comes to life. As this book was being assembled, C. Craig Venter and his team of molecular geneticists put synthetic DNA in a bacterium's cell which then began to replicate itself, a step closer to creating life.

In the play, the character of Galatea—an innocent born into in an adult woman's body—falls in love with her creator, Pygmalion. A moral crisis ensues when Pygmalion finds himself in the untenable position of having two almost identical wives. Moreover, he faces blindness if he breaks his vow of fidelity to Cynisca. Reading Gilbert's comedy today points to new biological, psychological, social, and ethical issues raised by the the recent sequencing of the genome and the explosion of stem cell research.

It is important to emphasize that cloning refers not mainly, as it does in the public's imagination and the media, to making identical copies of ourselves through the transfer of the DNA from a human cell into an egg cell with its DNA removed. Rather, the more immediate hopes for cloning consist of the capacity of undifferentiated stem cells to reproduce or copy themselves and change into adult cells, which comprise our various organs. In addition to this promise for regenerative medicine this process may one day even create alternate sources of fuel. Creating alternative fuel from cloned bacteria would be a greater benefit than the imagined dangers coming from the highly improbable creation of human clones. There are many today who see the cloning of even one human as comparable to creating Dr. Frankenstein's monster, an affront to the dignity of man. I find this a peculiar view if we acknowledge the indignities and atrocities we have committed and continue to commit during our short, approximately 200,000-year span on Earth or in the 20,000 or so years that we have told and retold the stories of these atrocities.

The first cloning of a mammal was accomplished with the sheep Dolly in Scotland in 1996 and is described by Dr. Jamie Love in his introduction to genetics (Chapter Six). His full course (www.synapses.co.uk/genetics/gene.html) is available on the internet. Stem cells, more importantly, are most promising in regenerative medicine with the possible repair of diseased tissues. For example, healthy pancreatic islet cells, derived from stem cells, might some day cure diabetes. Jonathan Shaw, the managing editor of *Harvard Magazine,* reviews the current state of stem-cell research (Chapter Seven).

Once mythologized as being created in the image of God in the Book of Genesis, in this book Homo sapiens is viewed as being shaped by nature and nurture. We are created in the images we have and expect of ourselves in the context of our complex unfolding evolution. In addition we have many inborn traits such as dependency, aggression, locomotion, curiosity, and procreation. Including our preliterate ancestors, we have inherited these traits over thousands of millennia. However, with the more recent acquisition of language (about 20,000 + years ago) and the transmission of knowledge orally, in writing, in print, and now digitally, our many human cultures evolve and define the rules and roles we play in our society. In contrast to our genetic inborn nature we call this latter "nurture," which, analogous to genes, also reproduces itself. The changes in nurture—our social environment—however, are evolving at a much faster pace from generation to generation and are further outpaced by the rate of technological change which is indeed challenging our capacity for adaptation.

This book exposes the reader to both the biological and socio-cultural reproduction of ourselves. In the context of social evolution Professor Carolyn Williams (Chapter Two) addresses the reproduction of male and female roles in the patriarchal setting of Victorian England when Gilbert wrote his play. We read her discussion with the hindsight of a century of changing male and female roles. What further changes can we imagine in the century ahead? For example, will men one day be able to bear children as Lee Silver speculates in his latest book, *Challenging Nature* (2006)? How long will it be before parents can choose the sex of their child genetically? We are already able to choose the gender of offspring by choosing among multiple embryos resulting from in vitro fertilization (IVF). The first successful test-tube baby, as mentioned earlier, was born in 1978 and is now in her thirties and in Generation X. Recently, in 2007, she conceived naturally and gave birth to a son. Robert Edwards, one of the developers of IVF, received a Nobel Prize in medicine as this book went to press.

Professor Lee Silver, in Chapter five, anticipates that with the rapid developments in technology a brave new world will soon be ours. In Chapter six, Bill McKibben cautions us as we move across the threshold of playing god by creating humans in our own images of them.

Art historian Tom Freudenheim (Chapter Three) reminds us that our species, since our cave dwelling days, has been reproducing and recording images of the world and and its inhabitants. as we experience and imagine it and one another. This was in spite of the warnings of Plato and the Old Testament commandment that we not create graven images.

Just as our myths, sciences, and art have evolved and defined us during the last two millennia, the new tools of genomic science tempt us again to move into uncharted territory. Biological engineering will raise questions and influence the answers to "what does it mean to be human?" How may or will humans change now that we have the tools of biogenetics along with the rapid growth of information technology?

BIBLIOGRAPHY

Borgman, J. (2000). "What are we going to do about the Y1K problem?" April, 1999; *Cincinnati Enquirer.*

Gilbert. W.S. (1876). *Original Plays*. London: Chatto and Windus.

Joshua, E. (2001). *Pygmalion and Galatea: The History of a Narrative in English Literature.* Aldershot: Ashgate.

Ovid (2004). *Metamorphoses.* Charles Martin, Ed., Transl., Introduction by Bernard Knox. New York: W.W. Norton.

Silver, L.M. (2007). *Challinging Nature: The Clash Between Biotechnology and Spirituality.* New York: Harper Perennial.

Chapter One
Psychoanalysis and the
Pygmalion-Galatea Process
Fred M. Sander, M.D.

W.S. Gilbert's version of the Pygmalion myth, *Pygmalion and Galatea* (1876), was his most successful play; it was also the last play he wrote before he began his famous collaboration with Arthur Sullivan. Gilbert's play is one of innumerable variations of the Pygmalion myth (Joshua, 2001). Ovid wrote the first version of this myth of transformation in the early years of the first millennium (Ovid/Knox, 2004). His Pygmalion, a sculptor unable to love any of the women on the island of Cyprus, created an ivory statue in his image of a perfect woman. He then fell in love with his creation. After Venus brought the statue to life, Pygmalion and his then unnamed creation married, had a child, and lived happily ever after. This two-thousand-year-old story of the creation of others in the images we have of them is the central theme of this book. Will the new technologies in the 21st century extend to cloning ourselves?

I PLOT SUMMARY[1]

In Gilbert's drama, Pygmalion is an Athenian sculptor living with his wife Cynisca. The marriage is happy, but childless. His wife also serves as his model, and his studio is filled with copies of her. It is as if he were surrounded by clones. When Cynisca informs Pygmalion she must leave him for a day, Pygmalion tells her that he will sorely miss her. She reminds him that if he feels lonely in her absence, he can find comfort in one of the many surrogates in his studio.

When Cynisca leaves, one of the copies of her—a stone image of a voluptuous woman—comes to life. As she becomes increasingly aware of herself as a living, breathing being, she falls in love with her creator Pygmalion. Pygmalion, who has bemoaned his inability to actually create life, is thrilled that his creation has indeed come

[1]In the following brief plot summary I have omitted two subplots unnecessary for the subsequent discussion.

to life and declares, "O woman—perfect in thy loveliness!"(p. 44).[2]
When Galatea learns from Pygmalion that she is a woman, she also
learns that he is married, and that he loves, and is loved by, his
wife. Galatea, in her innocence, declares, "Then I will [also] be thy
wife" (p. 46). Pygmalion informs her, however, that "the gods
allow but one" (p. 46).

The plot thickens as Pygmalion, taken by Galatea's beauty, sits
"sinfully" with her. Before Pygmalion and Cynisca married, they
had vowed to the goddess Artemis that if one of them should prove
unfaithful the other would gain the power to blind the "backslider."
Pygmalion's infidelity violates his vow. Cynisca, upon her return,
shocked and angered when his betrayal is revealed, blinds Pygmalion.

In the final act of the play the mayhem created by Galatea's birth is
satisfactorily resolved for Victorian audiences. Cynisca forgives
Pygmalion; his sight is restored, and Galatea, turned back into stone,
resumes her place on the pedestal from which she came to life.

This play was highly popular in the late 19th century. Female actors
of that era longed to play the role of the beautiful Galatea, though
uncertain how to interpret her character, with conflicting images of
innocence and sexuality. Audiences were titillated when they saw
the play, enjoying the portrayal of the satisfaction of forbidden
impulses. The reception of *Pygmalion and Galatea* underscores
just how much unconscious psychological needs and wishes affect
audiences—in other words, us.

II PSYCHOLOGY IN *PYGMALION AND GALATEA*

Freud pointed out that audience members participate in theatrical
performances through their own desires and yearnings; their
fantasies are lived out somehow in the drama. The audience may,
for example, identify with Galatea's wish to seduce her creator.

---

[2]Here, and subsequently, page numbers refer to this volume.

Or they may identify with Pygmalion's wish both to create and "sin" with his creation, despite his love for his wife. Freud wrote, "being present as an interested spectator at a play does for adults what play does for children. . . . Accordingly, his (the spectator's) enjoyment is based on an illusion . . . " (pp. 305–306). The Victorian audiences, although strict in their morality and certainly cognizant of the seriousness of sexual transgressions, nevertheless had unconscious needs to break down these restrictions. They were able to take vicarious enjoyment in Pygmalion and Galatea's "sinning" and "sitting lovingly together." Galatea, however, had to pay for her wanting to be Pygmalion's wife in having to return to stone and her pedestal. The characters in a play act out the audiences' forbidden desires and suffer the guilt and consequences associated with these desires. Turning an analytic lens onto Gilbert's play, I will introduce some of the core concepts of psychoanalytic theory that were already present in the first quarter of the 20th century. Some of these concepts are directly mirrored and dramatized, as if anticipated by Gilbert, which is in keeping with Freud's crediting artists with having portrayed and illuminated unconscious mental life long before the arrival of psychoanalysis.

One of the central insights of psychoanalysis is the importance of the role of early childhood experiences and fantasies, and how they are repressed, repeated or transformed in adult life. Quite revolutionary at the time, Freud grouped these early childhood wishes under the term "infantile sexuality." The previously assumed innocence of childhood was questioned as Freud saw the infant/child as having sexual and aggressive impulses. Galatea, as a child in a sexually adult female body, specifically dramatizes this idea.

One of the starting points of psychoanalytic theory is the centrality of the "Oedipus complex" which Freud considered universal in child development. The term originally came from Sophocles' play *Oedipus Rex*. Oedipus blinds himself upon discovering that he had married his mother and killed his father. Shocking at the time,

Fred M. Sander, M.D.

Freud stated that all children had strong feelings of love and hatred for their parents. A boy's love for his mother and rivalry with his father was paralleled by a similar dynamic in girls, who wanted to marry their fathers and displace their mothers. As indicated in the plot summary above, Pygmalion must tell Galatea that her wish to be his wife is forbidden by the gods. Such wishes from childhood become largely repressed and unconscious in the adult. Galatea's wish to marry her creator (father) was explicit and had to be socially suppressed and psychologically repressed. She is punished for this wish, fearing a return to stone, as she falls into a dream state (described below), and Pygmalion, in his participation, is blinded for his unfaithfulness.

As is true for many children, when Galatea first experiences sunset, darkness creates a separation from reality; with nighttime come dreams and, at times, nightmares. It is the time when one's unconscious mental life is especially active. With the arrival of night, Galatea, housed in Pygmalion's sister Myrine's home, feels that she has returned to stone, and then has a wish-fulfilling dream of a reunion with Pygmalion. I quote her account of falling asleep, dreaming and reawaking in full, as it is so evocative (pp. 53–54):

GALATEA'S DREAM

GALATEA: And then I sat alone and wept—and wept
          A long, long time for my Pygmalion.
          Then by degrees, by tedious degrees,
          The light—the glorious light!—the god-sent light!
          I saw it sink—sink—sink—behind the world!
          Then I grew cold—cold—as I used to be.
          Before, my loved Pygmalion gave me life.
          Then came the fearful thought that, by degrees,
          I was returning into stone again!
          How bitterly I wept and prayed aloud
          That it might not be so! "Spare me, ye gods!
          Spare me," I cried, "for my Pygmalion.

"A little longer for Pygmalion!
"Oh, take me not so early from my love;
"Oh, let me see him once—but once again!"
But no—they heard me not, for they are good,
And had they heard, must needs have pitied me;
They had not seen *thee,* and they did not know
The happiness that I must leave behind.
I fell upon thy couch (*to MYRINE*); my eyelids closed;
My senses faded from me one by one
I knew no more until I found myself,
After a strange dark interval of time,
Once more upon my hated pedestal,
A statue—motionless—insensible;
And then I saw the glorious gods come down!
Down to this room! The air was filled with them!
They came and looked upon Pygmalion,
And, looking on him, kissed him one by one,
And said, in tones that spoke to me of life,
"We cannot take her from such happiness!
"Live, Galatea, for his love!" And then
The glorious light that I had lost came back—
There was Myrine's room, there was her couch,
There was the sun in heaven; and the birds
Sang once more in the great green waving trees;
As I had heard them sing—I lived once more
To look on him I love!

MYRINE: Twas but a dream!
Once every day this death occurs to us,
Till thou and I and all who dwell on earth
Shall sleep to wake no more!

GALATEA: To wake no more?

PYGMALION: That time must come—may be not yet awhile—
Still it must come, and we shall all return
To the cold earth from which we quarried thee.

Her wish of reunion with Pygmalion fulfilled, she awakens at Myrine's home. Upon waking she also learns, however, that she must, like all mortals, face her own mortality.

In 1900, thirty years after *Pygmalion and Galatea* was first performed, Freud published his *Interpretation of Dreams*, an exploration of the depths of the unconscious mind. Galatea has but one day and night of life in Gilbert's play. Though dreams are more complexly understood today, Gilbert's account of Galatea's dream comes close to Freud's early citing of dreams as wish fulfillments and, at times, punishment for those wishes.

In addition to people's conflicted oedipal yearnings, Freud subsequently described what he called an earlier (pre-oedipal) narcissistic stage of development. This narcissistic love is vividly attested to by Galatea early in the play, before she realizes that she is a woman and unsure of the nature of her love for Pygmalion. He asks her about the "symptoms" of her love. She replies:

> A sense that I am made *by* thee *for* thee;
> That I've no will that is not wholly thine;
> That I've no thought, no hope, no enterprise
> That does not own thee as its sovereign;
> That I have life, that I may live for *thee,*
> That I am thine—that thou and I are one! (p. 46).

Her sense of the merging with Pygmalion, being a part of him, is how Freud saw an infant's earliest relationship with its mother before the infant becomes more autonomous. Galatea realizes that, separate from Pygmalion, as a woman unable to marry him, she nontheless feels rivalrous toward Cynisca. Galatea openly wonders if she is the fairest of her gender. To this end, Pygmalion hands her a mirror. Like Narcissus looking at himself in a pond, she falls in love with her own image, saying:

> How beautiful! I'm very glad to know
> That both our tastes agree so perfectly;
> Why, my Pygmalion, I did not think
> That aught could be more beautiful than thou,
> Till I beheld myself. Believe me, love,
> I could look in this mirror all day long.
> So I'm a woman! (p. 47).[3]

She is even happier to know she is a woman and states, "I'm glad I am a woman" (p. 45) after Pygmalion describes a male's role in their society:

> A being strongly framed,
> To wait on woman, and protect her from
> All ills that strength and courage can avert;
> To work and toil for her, that she may rest;
> To weep and mourn for her, that she may laugh;
> To fight and die for her, that she may live! (p. 45).

Here, we might wonder whether Gilbert is being ironical in mocking the disparity and reproduction of the idealized gender roles in Victorian England discussed by Professor Williams in the chapter following the play.

In addition to oedipal love and narcissistic self-love, Freud wrote about the child's painful discovery of sexual differences. Freud's "anatomy is destiny" concept may have reflected the disparity of gender roles in the pre-modern era and became highly controversial. Nonetheless, he felt it one of the normal psychological traumas of childhood. Two others were losing the person (usually the mother) one is first so dependent on, or losing her love.

Following this, the infant/toddler begins to feel inferior to its much larger parents who control their socialization during the stage of development referred to as toilet training. During these years the

[3]cf. Frontispiece on Freud's 1914 description of the forms of narcissistic love.

child develops a sense of self and individual identity through mimicking, mirroring and identifying with the images of its parents and the other people in their world. Images of oneself as being inferior or of being omnipotently superior alternate as the child slowly evolves into a self separate from its caretakers and develops a sense of reality. Even as adults, however, these feelings follow us. For example, Pygmalion feels pangs of separation when his wife first leaves him for a day: "It will be dark with me till you return" (p. 41). Later, he imagines the gods saying he "shall be the greatest among men, and yet infinitesimally small" (p. 42). When Pygmalion first tells Galatea she must go to his sister's house, her reponse is described in the stage direction as being, *"astonished and alarmed,"* almost like a child's painful first day of nursery school, she says, "Send me not hence, Pygmalion—let me stay" (p. 50).

Added to the above normal traumas of childhood there is castration anxiety linked to punishments for the already mentioned oedipal wishes, symbolically enacted as Pygmalion is blinded when he breaks his vow of fidelity, and when Galatea has the fearful thought in her dreamlike state that she is returned to stone. Finally, Freud also described the universal anxiety coming from our failure to live up to our own consciences, in the images most of us develop of our moral selves. Almost all the early findings of Freud are thus foreshadowed in Gilbert's 19th-century comedy.

III THE PYGMALION-GALATEA PROCESS

As a psychoanalyst who has taught and practiced analytically oriented couple and family therapy for over four decades, I have heard my patients again and again express the wish that the person(s) they are living with change in accordance with the images they have of each other. At almost every stage of family development, couples, as well as parents and their children, often repeat and deal with the conflicts of their early development.

Just as Pygmalion resisted Cynisca's leaving him for a day, couples struggle over conflicts around dependency, closeness, distance and autonomy. In addition, conflicts over dominance and submission, jealousy, adulterous wishes, guilt and punishment also manifest themselves in couples and families. Along with the tendency to unconsciously repeat experiences of childhood, there is also frequent blaming of the other for disappointments in their expectations: that the other person is not reflecting some preexisting image. I have called this reciprocal process the Pygmalion-Galatea Process (2004a). In this reciprocal process what is *in the mind* is also interpersonal.

About ten years ago this awareness of the Pygmalion myth as capturing the overt nature of many family relationships furthered my attempts to integrate psychoanalytic theory with couple and family therapy (1979; 1989). I shall illustrate, with a brief case vignette, one of any number of couples I have seen who present with the wish to change each other in one way or another. I have left out identifying details of the couple whom I saw many years ago. They and their immediate families would be the only ones able to recognize this vignette.

Larry and Louise, each about 40 years old, came because they could not resolve their conflict over whether to have a third child. The marriage hung in the balance. Louise insisted they have a third child. Larry was opposed. She came from an affluent family of three, and insisted on also having three children.

Larry, an only child from an economically disadvantaged family, exclaimed unequivocally, "No!" They both began with the expectation that the other would accommodate themselves to their images of what the family structure ought to be. This was but the tip of an iceberg of relational conflicts in which they expected the other to fit various images they had of the other. For example, Louise had an intense dislike of her father's strongly dominant style of family management. Although she bridled at her father's arbitrariness, she had identified with her father's dominance. She was quite discontent whenever Larry differed from her. She experienced such differences as a repetition of the dominance battle with her father, wanting Larry to take the submissive role her father put her in. Larry's father had held two jobs to support his family. He was not a hands-on father. In part, as a response to his childhood experience, Larry was a more involved father with his children; he also complained about Louise's demanding work schedule which reminded him of his father's time away from home. Now Larry was unwilling to take on yet more child care responsibilities, given what having a third child would mean.

Beneath these layers was a wish that their own mothers had been warmer. They both felt maternally deprived and both identified with their mothers' lack of warmth. This led to the distance in their relationship that made resolving their differences difficult. Their wishes for greater closeness went unmet. They each kept their distance—thus creating a repetitive self-fulfilling feeling of a depriving relationship.

This brief vignette illustrates the nature of Pygmalion-Galatea attempts to form or experience the other in one's image of him or her, and how these images were pre-determined by their relationships with their parents. Put slightly differently, the internal worlds of their childhoods were played out in the Pygmalion Processes of their adult lives.

The Pygmalion-Galatea Process tends to emphasize pathological or self-serving attempts to change others according to images one has of them. Such attempts may also be represented in positive images or expectations. This, however, can also be self-centered: for example, in a parent's attempt to guide or coerce an offspring to become a "chip off the old block" or to succeed where parents may feel they, themselves, have failed. In such instances the Pygmalion Process may be more coercive than caring. What may seem positive or well-intentioned to the parent may feel like coercion to the child because the child needs to grow up to be him- or herself, not a creation of the parents.

On the other hand, educators, parents and societies may also influence or inspire others in positive ways that are congruent with the ideals of individual students, children, family members, as well as groups. Quite recently social psychologists have named the process of such positive influence the Michelangelo Phenomenon (cf. a review by Rusbult, CE, et al. [2009]). Michelangelo's view of finding the real statue within the block of stone is invoked as a generative process in contrast to the narcissistic motive, for example, of Pygmalion's attempt, in Ovid's version, to create his image of a perfect woman. In Gilbert's play Pygmalion says:

> Give me a block of senseless marble—Well
> I'm a magician, and it rests with me
> To say what seedling lies within its shell; (p. 42).

Is this an instance of the Pygmalion Process or the Michaelangelo Phenomenon? In Gilbert's play Pygmalion felt he could do no more than imitate life, so in the above quote there is no agenda other than to "say" or fantasize that the statues are copies of his wife. What might his motive be, besides competing with the gods, in imagining his statues coming to life? The possibility that he had a fantasy that the statue might protect him against the possible loss of his wife also has some credence. The statue comes to life just after Cynisca leaves, and after she tells him he could turn to one of her surrogates when she is away. Many have theorized that the creation of art serves a reparative function in dealing with loss.

Throughout Gilbert's play the growing "seedling" copy of Cynisca, Galatea, like all children with minds of their own, tries to actualize her childish wishes, while Pygmalion tries to get her to accept the rules of their society.

MORE EXAMPLES IN DRAMAS

In addition to seeing this dynamic in couples and families, I began to recognize it in a number of dramatizations of the Pygmalion myth, or what seemed to me transparent versions of it. Mark

Fred M. Sander, M.D.

Medoff's *Children of a Lesser God* (1980) was the first. In this play James Leeds, a teacher, and Sarah Norman, his deaf student, fight over her autonomy as he tries to enforce the school's policy of teaching the students to speak rather than to use sign language. In a 1983 paper about this play I showed that James's ambivalent attraction to his deaf student was due in part to his own mother's verbal barrages, and the expectation that he be her savior. "I had to stop hearing her" (pp. 17–18), he says. In having a student who refused to speak (a reverse image of his mother), he sought to control her by teaching her how to speak. Sarah complained that he, like God, in the Book of Genesis, was trying to make her over in his own image. When they discuss their future marriage, Sarah insists that they have deaf children who sign, in the image of herself.

In *Children of a Lesser God,* centered around questions of communication and learning to speak, I noticed the obvious resemblance to G.B. Shaw's *Pygmalion* (1913). In Shaw's play, Henry Higgins attempts to change Eliza Doolittle from a cockney flower girl into a duchess (Weissman, P., 1958; Levine, S., 2001). At one point Higgins tells his mother, "you have no idea how frightfully interesting it is to take a human being and change her into a quite different human being by creating a new speech for her" (p. 327).

The process is not, as Higgins at first intends, one way; Eliza Doolittle actually comes to Higgins's laboratory prepared to pay for speech lessons. During the course of the lessons she also has an influence on him: he softens and begins to care more personally for her. Nonetheless, she leaves him at the end to marry Freddy, someone less controlling than Higgins whom *she* can, in fact, more likely control.

I then saw the most recent direct adaptation of the Pygmalion myth, Neil LaBute's (2001) *The Shape of Things* in which Eve, an art student, convinces her naive boyfriend, Adam, to radically change his appearance. At the end of the play she presents Adam as her art project, in the image she had of him, to her faculty. Adam sits in the audience stunned to discover that Evelyn had objectified rather than loved him. In this adaptation of the Pygmalion myth, the gender roles of Pygmalion and Galatea are reversed.[4]

At this juncture I began to research the Pygmalion myth and came upon Gilbert's play which, like a statue in theatrical archives, was buried for nearly a century. I was so impressed with its current resonance that I "brought it to life" in a staged public reading in 2003 (Sander, 2004b). I continued to see the universality of the Pygmalion-Galatea Process present in most individuals, especially in couples and families seeking help.

The Pygmalion Process begins in everyone's early development as each person first learns communication skills by mirroring, mimicking and identifying with their parents' and others' words and gestures. Of course, this language development is made more complex when children learn to say "no," a word they actually first learn from their parents (Spitz, 1957). They begin to have minds of their own. We can recall here the actual "no" of my patient, Larry, as well as Sarah, in Mark Medoff's play, and additionally in Eliza Doolittle's intermittent resistance to Higgins's efforts. Only Adam in *The Shape of Things* remained compliant.

MYTHS IN PSYCHOLOGICAL THEORY

Our species is a myth making one (Murray, H., 1960). In fact myth making is itself an example of the Pygmalion Process. Stories told, retold, copied, and redefined were first transmitted orally about 20,000 years ago. There followed script, print, audio-visual and now digital recordings. W.S. Gilbert's adaptation of the Pygmalion myth is one of hundreds of adaptations of this particular creation myth (Joshua, 2001). Essaka Joshua quotes Levi-Strauss's (1965) comment about the Oedipus myth to emphasize that all myths are redefined in changing contexts:

---

[4]In an 1883 burlesque of Gilbert's play, *Galatea or Pygmalion Reversed* (Stevens, HP, et al.), Pygmalion was a female and Galatea her lazy husband.

"It cannot be too strongly emphasized that all variants
[of a myth] should be taken into account. [...] There is
no true version of which all the others are but copies or
distortions. Every version belongs to the myth" (p. xix).

The Pygmalion myth is itself one of countless other myths we have
created after *homo-sapiens* learned to think, speak and seek meaning in our lives. The evolution of such cultural forms, called memes,
are similar to the evolution or spread of genes according to Richard
Dawkins (1976).

Freud, as he developed the individual treatment modality of psychoanalysis, used two Greek myths (Oedipus and Narcissus) to support
his clinical explorations of the individual's sexual and unconscious
conflicts. These myths, though tales of interpersonal struggles, came
to represent, in Freudian theory, the power of wishes and conflicts
within the individual. Freud focused on his patients' internal
conflicts. In working with couples and families it is an interpersonal framework that is primary. Individuals, marital partners,
parents, children and almost all of society's institutions are agents
attempting, in light of the images and expectations of others, to
influence or transform them. The Pygmalion-Galatea Process
emphasizes that forming transferences is ubiquitous in relationships,
and especially pronounced in couples and families. From the earliest days of psychoanalysis these tendencies, defined as transferences,
were analyzed in the dyadic setting of the patient and analyst.

The therapeutic process and the analytic process are also examples
of the Pygmalion-Galatea Process. Freud was quite aware of the role
of suggestion in psychotherapy, especially during the time he was
experimenting with hypnosis. With the development of psychoanalytic technique he tried to minimize this educational function
while analyzing the patients' defenses against unacceptable impulses
and the transference distortions in their images of their analysts.
Nonetheless, Jerome Frank (1961) noted the inevitable role of influence in all psychotherapies. There are unconscious factors at play

in any therapeutic encounter. Shelley Orgel (1991) warned against the danger of psychotherapists or psychoanalysts consciously or unconsciously creating the patient or patients in their own images. This view implies a one-way process, though we now appreciate the two-person interaction in all dyadic relationships. Susan Levine's (2001) study of Shaw's *Pygmalion* notes that analysts and their patients often enact fantasies of creation and rebirth (p. 104) which we might see as a "cautionary parable" for psychoanalysis.

IV THE CONTEMPORARY RESONANCE OF W.S. GILBERT'S *PYGMALION AND GALATEA*

Ovid's version of the Pygmalion myth, tells the tale of a sculptor who created and fell in love with his perfect creation. This is a patriarchal myth of man's creation of a woman as in Eve's creation out of Adam's rib in the *Book of Genesis*. The popular version, G.B. Shaw's *Pygmalion*, further adapted by Lerner and Loewe in the even more popular *My Fair Lady* (1956), captures our universal attempts to create others in the images we have of them by altering their speech and language. At one level Shaw was expressing his disapproval of the English class system. Its popularity beyond this, however, owes much to its tapping into the experience of how we come to be who we are, by mimicking our parents and teachers, and rebelling against them. Shaw's version of the myth, devoid of the gods, heroes and monsters of the past, may be best suited for our secular and scientific age.

Gilbert's *Pygmalion and Galatea* was buried for almost a century. Why bring this forgotten comedy back to life? The story anticipates psychoanalytic theory which grew out of the same Victorian soil as Gilbert's play. The republication of Gilbert's play, with the essays to follow, also allows us to reflect upon how we, as a species, are always replicating ourselves. The new age of stem cell genomic medicine, cloning, simultaneously converging with digital replication has arrived. How will we deal with it?

That Pygmalion, in Gilbert's play, sought god-like powers serves to remind us of our creation myths. In our secular times, rather than being created in God's image, we are now on the frontier, with the appearance of new molecular technologies, of creating ourselves in our own images in ways that have never before been possible (Silver, 1997, 2006). Before the 21st century this was only barely imaginable as, for example, in Mary Shelley's *Frankenstein* (1818 [1977]).

How will we use these new technologies? How will we use stem cell research; the life-creating and healing powers that are now in our hands? How will we decide? Much will depend on human nature, so consistently resistant to change, with or without our deities during our short twenty-to-thirty-thousand-year tenure on this planet. What are we looking to today?

In response to Cynisca's suggestion that in her absence he turn to one of the copies of her, Pygmalion, still under the sway of his image of the gods, with his ambition and vulnerability, his reach exceeding his grasp, states:

> The thing is but a statue after all!"
> Cynisca little thought that in those words
> [*that he seek comfort in his lifeless creation*].
>
> She touched the key-note of my discontent—
> True, I have powers denied to other men;
> Give me a block of senseless marble—Well
> I'm a magician, and it rests with me
> To say what seedling lies within its shell;
> It shall contain a man, a woman—child—
> A dozen men and women if I will.
> So far the gods and I run neck and neck;
> Nay, so far I can beat them at their trade!
> *I* am no bungler—all the men I make
> Are straight-limbed fellows, each magnificent

In the perfection of his manly grace:
I make no crook-backs—all my men are gods,
My women goddesses—in outward form.
But there's my tether! I can go so far,
And go no farther! At that point I stop,
To curse the bonds that hold me sternly back:
To curse the arrogance of those proud gods,
Who say, "Thou shall be greatest among men,
"And yet infinitesimally small!" (p. 42).

Almost a century after Gilbert penned these lines, Watson and Crick (1953) discovered, during some of our lifetimes, the building block of life in the double helix structure of DNA (1953). Soon after this discovery, the first stem cell was described (1973). About the same time the first in vitro fertilization was accomplished (1978). Since then we have begun to clone animals—for example, the sheep Dolly, described in Chapter Six.

By 2002 the human genome, with its 25–30,000 genes and 3 billion DNA bases, had been sequenced. Coincidentally, this year, 2010, C. Craig Venter and his team made it possible for a bacterium to replicate itself after they inserted synthetic DNA into another enucleated bacterium. Technically, this was not creating life as the enucleated cell was still "natural."

To follow is the original text of the 1876 Gilbert play with slight changes, rendering archaic language into current vernacular and adding a supplemental ending. I also added the reason for Cynisca's departure for a day, her intent to seek help from Artemis, the goddess of fertility, for her childless state.

The new ending, following Galatea's return to stone, facilitates an improvisational enactment with the audience, of assisted reproductive technology (ART), an advance short of—but soon to merge with—biogenetic engineering. Cynisca, yearning for a daughter, seeks a sperm- or egg-donor, a faith-assissted pregnancy, an adoption, or a clone. A shortened version of the central plot, eliminating two subplots, can be found on the website: www.Createdinourownimages.com.

This could then be followed by either panel or audience discussions of the issues we face in the age of the genome—those raised in this book. After the following play, a number of essays address some of the issues evoked by *Pygmalion and Galatea,* all with the purpose of continuing the discussion, dialogues, and debates that will occupy all of us in our digital age of the genome.

BIBLIOGRAPHY

Dawkins, R. (1976). *The Selfish Gene.* Oxford: Oxford University Press.

Frank, J. (1961). *Persuasion and Healing: A Comparative Study of Psychotherapy.* Baltimore: Johns Hopkins Press.

Freud, S. (1907). Psychopathic Characters on the Stage. Standard Edition, VII, pp. 305–306. London: Hogarth Press.

Gilbert, W.S. (1876). *Original Plays.* London: Chatto and Windus.

Joshua, E. (2001). Pygmalion and Galatea: The History of a Narrative in English Literature.

LaBute, N. (2001). *The Shape of Things.* London: Faber and Faber.

Lerner, A.J., and Loewe, F. (1956). *My Fair Lady.*

Levine, S.S. (2001). On the Mirror Stage with Henry and Eliza or Play-ing with *Pygmalion* in Five Acts. *Journal of Applied Psychoanalysis,* Vol 3, No. 2.

Medoff, M. (1980). *Children of a Lesser God.* New York: Dramatists Play Service.

Murray, H. (ed.) 1960. *Myth and Myth Making.* New York: G. Braziller.

Ovid. (1963). *Metamorphoses* Vol. 2 Miller, F.J. transl. Cambridge, MA. Harvard University Press.

Sander, F.M. (1979). *Individual and Family Therapy: Toward an Integration.* Northvale, NJ: Jason Aronson.

———— (1983). Communication and the Development of Autonomy: Reflections on *Children of a Lesser God* by Mark Medoff, (1980) *International Journal of Family Psychiatry*. Vol. 4, No. 4, p. 277–293.

———— (2004a). Psychoanalytic Couple Therapy: Classical Style. *Psychoanalytic Inquiry* Vol 24, No.3, pp. 373–386.

———— (2004b). The Discovery and Revival of W.S. Gilbert's *Pygmalion and Galatea*. Billingham, England: *The Gaiety.*

Shaw, G.B. (1913 [2002]). *Plays*, Second Edition. New York: W.W. Norton.

Shelley, M. (1818 [1977]). The Annotated *Frankenstein* (italics). Ed. Leonard Woollf. New York: Clarkson N. Potter.

Spitz, R. (1957). *Yes and No: On the genesis of communication.* New York: International Universities Press.

Stephens, HP, Webster, W. (1883) *Galatea or Pygmalion Re-versed.* London: H. Blacklock and Co.

Levi-Strauss, C. (1965). *The Structural Study of Myth: A Symposium,* ed. by Thomas a Sebeok (Bloomington, Indiana), p. 95.

Watson, J.D. and Crick, F. (1953). Molecular Structure of Nucleic Acids. *Nature* 164:1537–1539.

Weissman, P. (1958). Shaw's Childhood and *Pygmalion. Psychoanalytic Study of the Child,* 13:541–561.

PYGMALION AND GALATEA

An Original Mythological Comedy
IN THREE ACTS

By W.S. Gilbert

With minimal revisions and
a supplemental ending
by Fred M. Sander, M.D. (2003)

Published London: Chatto and Windus, 1876

First produced at the Haymarket Theatre,
  9 December, 1871

DRAMATIS PERSONAE

PYGMALION, *an Athenian Sculptor* ....Mr. Kendal

LEUCIPPE, *a Soldier* ....Mr. Howe

CHRYSOS *an Art Patron* ....Mr. Buckstone

AGESIMOS, *Chrysos's Slave* ....Mr. Braid

MIMOS, *Pygmalion's Slave* ....Mr. Weathersby

GALATEA, *an Animated Statue* ....Miss M. Robertson

CYNISCA, *Pygmalion's wife* ....Miss Caroline Hill

DAPHNE, *Chrysos's Wife* ....Mrs. Chippendale

MYRINE, *Pygmalion's Sister* ....Miss Merton

SCENE: PYGMALION'S STUDIO

The action is comprised within the space of twenty-four hours

PYGMALION AND GALATEA
ACT I
SCENE: PYGMALION'S STUDIO

[*Several classical statues are placed about the room; at the back a temple or cabinet containing a statue of* GALATEA, *before which curtains are drawn concealing the statue from the audience.*]

[MIMOS, *a slave, is discovered at work on a half-finished statue. To him enters* AGESIMOS.]

AGESIMOS (*haughtily*): Good day. Is this Pygmalion's studio

MIMOS (*bowing*): It is.

AGESIMOS: Are you Pygmalion?

MIMOS: Oh, no;
    I am his slave.

AGESIMOS: And has Pygmalion slaves!
    A sculptor with a slave to wait on him:
    A slave to fetch and carry—come and go—
    And p'raps a whip to thrash him if he don't!
    What's the world coming to?

MIMOS: What is your will?

AGESIMOS: This: Chrysos will receive Pygmalion
    At half-past three to day; so bid him come.

MIMOS: And are you Chrysos, sir?

AGESIMOS (*disconcerted*): Well, no I'm not.
    That is not altogether: I'm, in fact,
    His slave.

MIMOS (*relieved*): His slave!

AGESIMOS (*very proudly*): My name's Agesimos!

MIMOS: And has Agesimos a master then,
           To bid him fetch and carry—come and go—
           And wield a whip to thrash him if he don't?
           What's the world coming to!

AGESIMOS: Poor purblind fool!
           I'd sooner tie the sandals of my lord,
           Than own five hundred thousand such as you.
           Whip! Why Agesimos would rather far
           Be whipped by Chrysos seven times a day,
           Than whip you hence to the Acropolis;
           What say you now?

MIMOS: Why that upon one point
           Aegesimos and I are quite agreed.
           And who is Chrysos?

AGESIMOS: Hear the slave, ye gods!
           He knows not Chrysos!

MIMOS: Indeed, not I.

AGESIMOS: He is the chiefest man in Athens, sir;
           The patron of the arts—a nobleman
           Of princely liberality and taste,
           On whom five hundred starved Pygmalions
           May feed on if they will.

               (*Enter PYGMALION.*)

PYGMALION: Who is this man?

AGESIMOS: I'm Chrysos's slave—my name's Agesimos.
        Chrysos has heard of you: he understands
        That you have talent, and he condescends
        To bid you call on him. But take good care
        How you offend him: he can make or mar.

PYGMALION: Your master's slave reflects his insolence!
Tell him from me that, though I'm poor enough,
I am an artist and a gentleman.
He should not reckon Art among his slaves:
She rules the world—so let him wait on her.

AGESIMOS: You are a sculptor!

PYGMALION: (*furiously*). And an angry one!
Begone, and take my message to your lord.
(*Exit AGESIMOS*)
Insolent hound!

(*Enter CYNISCA.*)

CYNISCA: Pygmalion, what's amiss?

PYGMALION: Chrysos has sent his slave to render me
The customary tribute paid by wealth
To mere intelligence.

CYNISCA: Pygmalion!
Brooding upon the prescribed insolence
Of a mere slave! Dismiss the thought at once.
Come, take thy chisel; thou hast work to do
Ere thy wife-model takes her leave to-day;
In half-an-hour I must be on the road
To Athens. Half-an-hour remains to thee—
Come—make the most of it—I'll pose myself;
Say—will that do?

PYGMALION: I cannot work to-day.
My hand's uncertain—I must rest awhile.

CYNISCA: Then rest and gaze upon thy masterpiece,
'Twill reconcile thee to thyself—Behold!

(*Draws curtain and discovers statue of* GALATEA.)

PYGMALION: Yes—for in gazing on my handiwork,
        I gaze on heaven's handiwork—thyself!

CYNISCA: And yet, although it be thy masterpiece,
        It has the fault thy patrons find with all
        Thy many statues.

PYGMALION: What then do they say?

CYNISCA: They say Pygmalion's statues have one head—
        That head, Cynisca's is mine.

PYGMALION: So then it's a fault
        To reproduce one hundred thousand fold,
        For the advantage of mankind at large,
        The happiness the gods have given me!
        Well, when I find a fairer head than thine
        I'll give my patrons some vairiety.

CYNISCA: I would not have thee find another head
        That seemed as fair to thee for all the world!
        We'll have no stranger models if you please,
        I'll be your model, sir, as heretofore,
        So reproduce me at your will; and yet
        It were sheer vanity in me to think
        This fair stone recalls Cynisca's face!

PYGMALION: Cynisca's face in every line!

CYNISCA: No, no!
        Those outlines softened, angles smoothed away,
        The eyebrows arched, the head more truly poised,
        The forehead ten years smoother than mine own,
        Tell rather of Cynisca as she was
        When, in the silent groves of Artemis,
        Pygmalion told his love ten years ago:
        And then the placid brow, the sweet sad lips,
        The gentle head down-bent resignedly,
        Proclaim that this is not Pygmalion's wife,
        Who laughs and frowns, but knows no compromise.
        I am no longer as that statue is! (*Closes curtains.*)

PYGMALION: Why here's ingratitude, to slander Time,
           Who in his hurried course has passed thee by!
           Or is it that Cynisca won't allow
           That Time could pass her by, and never pause
           To print a kiss upon so fair a face?

(Enter MYRINE)

MYRINE: Pygmalion; I have news.

PYGMALION: My sister, speak.

MYRINE: *(bashfully)* Send Mimos hence.

PYGMALION *(signs to Mimos)*: Now we are quite alone.

MYRINE: Leucippe—

CYNISCA: Well!

MYRINE *(to Pygmalion)*: He was thy schoolfellow,
           And thou and he are brothers save in blood;
           He loves my brother as a brother.

PYGMALION: Yes, I'm sure of that; but is that all thy news?
           There's more to come!

MYRINE *(bashfully)*: He loves thy sister too.

PYGMALION: Why this is news, Myrine—kiss me girl.
           I'm more than happy at thy happiness,
           There is no better fellow in the world!

CYNISCA But tell us all about it, dear. How came
           The awkward, bashful, burly warrior,
           To nerve himself to this confession?

(LEUCIPPE appears at door.)

MYRINE: Why—
           He's here—and he shall tell thee how it was.

LEUCIPPE: In truth I hardly know! I'm new at it;
           I'm but a soldier. Could I fight my way

Into a maiden's heart, why well and good;
I'd get there, somehow. But to talk and sigh,
And whisper pretty things—I can't do that!
I tried it, but I stammered, blushed, and failed.
Myrine laughed at me—but, bless her heart,
She knew my meaning, and she pulled me through!

MYRINE: I don't know how, Pygmalion, but I did.
He stammered, as he tells you, and I laughed;
And then I felt so sorry, when I saw
The great, big, brave Leucippe look so like
A beaten schoolboy—that I think I cried.
And then—I quite forget what happened next,
Till, by some means, we, who had always been
So cold and formal, distant and polite,
Found ourselves—

LEUCIPPE: Each upon the other's neck!
You are not angry? (*offering his hand*).

PYGMALION: (*taking it*) Angry? overjoyed!
I wish I had been there, unseen, to see;
No sight could give me greater joy!

LEUCIPPE: What! say you so? Why then, Myrine, girl,

We'll reproduce it for his benefit. (They embrace.)
See here, Pygmalion, here's a group for thee!
Come, fetch thy clay, and set to work on it,
I'll promise thee thy models will not tire!

CYNISCA: How now, Leucippe, where's the schoolboy
blush
That used to coat thy face at sight of her?

LEUCIPPE: The coating was but thin, we've rubbed it off!

(*Kisses MYRINE.*)

PYGMALION: Take care of him, Myrine; thou hast not
The safeguard that protects her (*indicating CYNISCA*)

MYRINE: What is that?

CYNISCA: It's a strange story. Many years ago
          I was a holy nymph of Artemis,
          Pledged to eternal maidenhood!

LEUCIPPE: Indeed!

MYRINE: How terrible!

CYNISCA: It seemed not so to me;
          For weeks and weeks I pondered steadfastly
          Upon the nature of that serious step
          Before I took it—lay awake at night,
          Looking upon it from this point and that,
          And I at length determined that the vow,
          Which to Myrine seems so terrible,
          Was one that I, at all events, could keep.

MYRINE: How old wast thou, Cynisca?

CYNISCA: I was ten!
          Well—in due course, I reached eleven, still
          I saw no reason to regret the step;
          Twelve—thirteen—fourteen saw me still unchanged;
          At fifteen, it occurred to me one day
          That marriage was a necessary ill,
          Inflicted by the gods to punish us,
          And to evade it were impiety;
          E'en though faithlessness was wide.
          At sixteen the idea became more fixed;
          At seventeen I was convinced of it!

PYGMALION: In the mean time she'd seen Pygmalion.

MYRINE: And you confided all your doubts to him?

CYNISCA: I did, and he confirmed them—so we laid
          The case before my mistress Artemis;
          No need to tell the arguments we used,
          Suffice it that they brought about our end.
          And Artemis, her icy steadfastness

Thawed by the ardour of Cynisca's prayers,
Replied, "Go, girl, and wed Pygmalion;
"But mark my words, whichever one of you,
"Or he or she, shall falsify the vow
"Of perfect conjugal fidelity—
"The wronged one, he or she, shall have the power
"To call down blindness on the backslider,
"And sightless shall the truant mate remain
"Until expressly pardoned by the other."

LEUCIPPE: It's fortunate such powers as thine are not
In universal use; for if they were,
One-half the husbands and one-half the wives
Would be as blind as night; the other half,
Having their eyes, would use them—on each other!

(*MIMOS enters, and gives PYGMALION a scroll, which he reads.*)

MYRINE: But then, the power of calling down this doom
Remains with thee. Thou wouldst not burden him
With such a curse as utter sightlessness,
However grievously he might offend?

CYNISCA: I love Pygmalion for his faithfulness;
The act that robs him of that quality
Will rob him of the love that springs from it.

MYRINE: But sightlessness—it is so terrible!

CYNISCA: And faithlessness—it is so terrible!
I take my temper from Pygmalion;
While he is god-like—he's a god to me,
And should he turn to devil, I'll turn with him;
I know no half-moods, I am love or hate!

MYRINE (*to LEUCIPPE*): What do you say to that?

LEUCIPPE: Why, on the whole
I'm glad *you're* not a nymph of Artemis!
(*Exeunt MYRINE and LEUCIPPE.*)

PYGMALION: I've put his mind at ease.   Presently
    My patron Chrysos will be here to earn
    Some thousand drachmas.

CYNISCA: How, my love to earn?
    He is a man of unexampled wealth,
    And follows no profession.

PYGMALION: Yes, he does;
    He is a patron of the Arts, and makes
    A handsome income by his patronage.

CYNISCA: How so?

PYGMALION: He is an ignorant buffoon,
    But money holds a higher rank than brains,
    And he is rich; wherever Chrysos buys,
    The world of smaller fools comes following,
    And men are glad to sell their work to him
    At half its proper price, that they may say,
    "Chrysos has purchased handiwork of ours."
    He is a fashion, and he knows it well
    In buying sculpture; he appraises it
    As he'd appraise a master-mason's work—
    So much for marble, and so much for time,
    So much for working tools-but still he buys,
    And so he is a patron of the Arts!

CYNISCA: To think that heaven-born Art should be the slave
    Of such as he!

PYGMALION: Well, wealth is heaven-born too.
    I work for wealth.

CYNISCA: Thou workest, love, for fame.

PYGMALION: And fame brings wealth. The thought's con-
    temptible,
    But I can do no more than work-for wealth,.
    And also need a slave or two.

CYNISCA: Such words from one whose noble work it is
          To call the senseless marble into life!

PYGMALION: Life! Dost thou call that life
           (*Indicating statue of GALATEA.*)

CYNISCA: It all but breathes!

PYGMALION (*bitterly*): It all but breathes—therefore it
           talks aloud!
           It all but moves—therefore it walks and runs!
           It all but lives, and therefore it is life!
           No, no, you see, the thing is cold, dull stone,
           Shaped to a certain form, but still dull stone,
           The lifeless, senseless mockery of life.
           The gods make life: I can make only death!
           Why, my Cynisca, though I stand so well,
           The merest cut-throat, when he plies his trade,
           Makes better death than I, with all my skill!

CYNISCA: Hush, my Pygmalion! the gods are good,
          And they have made thee nearer unto them
          Than other men; this is ingratitude!

PYGMALION: Not so; has not a monarch's second son
            More cause for anger that he lacks a throne
            Than he whose lot is cast in slavery?

CYNISCA: Not more cause than I
          With no creation of my own.

PYGMALION: Again, you blame me for your woes.

CYNISCA: Now I must go.

PYGMALION: When will you return?

CYNISCA (*irritated*): What matter.
          You have your Art.
          I'll plead my case to Artemis
          And hopefully return tomorrow.

PYGMALION: So soon, and for so long!

CYNISCA: One day, 'twill quickly pass away!

PYGMALION: With those
　　　　　　Who measure time by almanacks, no doubt,
　　　　　　But not with him who knows no days save those
　　　　　　Born of the sunlight of Cynisca's eyes;
　　　　　　It will be dark with me till you return.

CYNISCA: Then sleep it through, Pygmalion! But stay,
　　　　　　Thou shalt *not* pass the weary hours alone;
　　　　　　Now mark thou this—while I'm away from thee,
　　　　　　There stands my only surrogate. (*Indicating*
　　　　　　GALATEA.)
　　　　　　She is my proxy, and I charge you, sir,
　　　　　　Into her quietly attentive ear
　　　　　　Pour all thy treasures of hyperbole,
　　　　　　And give thy nimble tongue full license, lest
　　　　　　Disuse should rust its glib machinery;
　　　　　　If thoughts of love should haply crowd on thee,
　　　　　　There stands my other self; tell them to her;
　　　　　　She'll listen well. (*He makes a movement of*
　　　　　　impatience.)
　　　　　　For she is I, yet lovelier than I,
　　　　　　And hath no temper, sir, and hath no tongue!
　　　　　　Thou hast thy art, make good use of it.
　　　　　　I'm half jealous of thy work—(*closes curtain*)
　　　　　　There, its gone.
　　　　　　The thing is but a statue after all,
　　　　　　And I am safe in leaving thee with it;
　　　　　　Farewell, Pygmalion, till I return.

(Exits without a kiss)

PYGMALION: "The thing is but a statue after all!"
　　　　　　Cynisca little thought that in those words
　　　　　　She touched the key-note of my discontent—

True, I have powers denied to other men;
Give me a block of senseless marble—Well
I'm a magician, and it rests with me
To say what seedling lies within its shell;
It shall contain a man, a woman—child—
A dozen men and women if I will.
So far the gods and I run neck and neck;
Nay, so far I can beat them at their trade!
I am no bungler—all the men I make
Are straight-limbed fellows, each magnificent
In the perfection of his manly grace:
I make no crook-backs—all my men are gods,
My women goddesses—in outward form.
But there's my tether! I can go so far,
And go no farther! At that point I stop,
To curse the bonds that hold me sternly back:
To curse the arrogance of those proud gods,
Who say, "Thou shall be greatest among men,
"And yet infinitesimally small!"

GALATEA. Pygmalion!

PYGMALION: Who called?

GALATEA: Pygmalion!

(*PYGMALION tears away curtain and discovers GALATEA alive.*)

PYGMALION: Ye gods! It lives!

GALATEA: Pygmalion!

PYGMALION: It speaks!
        I have my prayer! my Galatea breathes!

GALATEA: Where am I? Let me speak, Pygmalion:
        Give me thy hand—both hands—how soft and warm!
        Whence came I? (*Descends.*)

PYGMALION: Why, from yonder pedestal!

GALATEA: That pedestal? Ah, yes, I recollect,
There was a time when it was part of me.

PYGMALION: That time has passed for ever, thou art now
A living, breathing woman, excellent
In every attribute of womanhood.

GALATEA: "Attri-bute of womanhood? (*not seeming to understand*) Where am I, then?

PYGMALION: Why, born into this world (*spreads out arms to the outside*) By miracle!

GALATEA: "By Miracle?" (*puzzled*)
Is this the world? (*spreads out arms mirroring PYGMALION*)

PYGMALION: It is.

GALATEA: What is this? (*points to the inside*) This room?

PYGMALION: This room is portion of a house;
The house stands in a grove; the grove itself
Is one of many, many hundred groves
Here in Athens.

GALATEA: And is Athens then the world?

PYGMALION: To you and me, Athenians—Yes—

GALATEA: And I am one?

PYGMALION: You are my creation.

GALATEA: "You are my creation?"

PYGMALION: No,
I modelled you in clay—my artisans
Then roughed you out in marble quarried in Pentelicus;
I, in turn brought my artistic skill to bear on you,
And made you what you are—in all but life—
The gods completed what I had begun,
And gave the only gift I could not give!

GALATEA: Then this is life? (*spins around*)

PYGMALION: It is. (*dances with her*)

GALATEA: And not long since
        I was a cold, dull stone! I recollect
        That by some means I knew that I was stone:
        That was the first dull gleam of consciousness;
        I became conscious of a chilly self,
        A cold immovable identity,
        I knew that I was stone, and knew no more!
        Then, by an imperceptible advance,
        Came the dim evidence of outer things,
        Seen—darkly and imperfectly—yet seen—
        This room surrounding me, and I, alone.
        That pedestal—that curtain—then a voice
        That called out "Galatea!" At that word,
        Which seemed to shake my marble to the core,
        That which was dim before, came evident.
        Sounds, that had hummed around me, indistinct,
        Vague, meaningless—seemed to resolve themselves
        Into a language I could understand;
        I felt my frame pervaded by a glow
        That seemed to thaw my marble into flesh;
        Its cold hard substance throbbed with active life,
        My limbs grew supple, and I moved—I lived!
        Lived in the ecstasy of new-born life!
        Lived in the image of him that fashioned me!
        Lived in a thousand tangled thoughts of hope,
        Love, gratitude—thoughts that resolved themselves
        Into one word, that word, Pygmalion!
        (*kneels to him.*)

PYGMALION: I have no words to tell thee of my joy,
        O woman—perfect in thy loveliness!

GALATEA: What is that word? Am I a woman?

PYGMALION: Yes.

GALATEA: Art thou a woman?

PYGMALION: No, I am a man.
          But of woman born.

GALATEA: What *is* a man?

PYGMALION: A being strongly framed,
          To wait on woman, and protect her from
          All ills that strength and courage can avert;
          To work and toil for her, that she may rest;
          To weep and mourn for her, that she may laugh;
          To fight and die for her, that she may live!

GALATEA (*after a pause*): I'm glad I am a woman.

PYGMALION: So am I. (*They sit.*)

GALATEA: That I escape the pains thou hast to bear?

PYGMALION: That I may undergo those pains for thee.

GALATEA: With whom then wouldst thou fight?

PYGMALION: With any man
          Whose deed or word gave Galatea pain.

GALATEA: Then there are other men in this strange world?

PYGMALION: There are, indeed!

GALATEA: And other women?

PYGMALION (*taken aback*): Yes;
          Though for the moment I'd forgotten it!
          Yes, other women.

GALATEA: And for all of these
          Men work, and toil, and mourn, and weep, and
          fight?

PYGMALION: It is man's duty, if he's called upon,
          To fight for all—he works for those he loves

GALATEA: Then by thy work I know thou lovest me.

PYGMALION: Indeed, I love thee! (*Embraces her.*)

GALATEA: With what kind of love?

PYGMALION: I love thee (*recollecting himself and releasing her*)
        as a sculptor loves his work!
        (*aside*) There is a diplomacy in that reply.

GALATEA: My love is different in kind to thine:
        I am no sculptor, and I've done no work,
        Yet I do love thee: say—what love is mine?

PYGMALION: Tell me its symptoms, then I'll answer thee.

GALATEA: Its symptoms? Let me call them as they come.
        A sense that I am made *by* thee *for* thee;
        That I've no will that is not wholly thine;
        That I've no thought, no hope, no enterprise
        That does not own thee as its sovereign;
        That I have life, that I may live for *thee,*
        That I am thine—that thou and I are one!
        What kind of love is that?

PYGMALION: A kind of love
        That I shall run some risk in dealing with!

GALATEA: And why, Pygmalion?

PYGMALION: Such love as thine
        A man may not receive, except indeed
        From one who is, or is to be, his wife.

GALATEA: Then I will be thy wife!

PYGMALION: That may not be;
        I have a wife—the gods allow but one.

GALATEA: Why did the gods then send me here to thee?

PYGMALION: I cannot say—unless to punish me
        For unreflecting and presumptuous prayer!
        I prayed that thou shouldst live—I have my prayer,
        And now I see the fearful consequence
        That must attend it!

GALATEA: Yet thou lovest me?

PYGMALION: Who could look on that face and stifle love?

GALATEA: Then I am beautiful?

PYGMALION: Indeed thou art.

GALATEA: I wish that I could look upon myself,
        But that's impossible.

PYGMALION: Not so Indeed.
        This mirror will reflect thy face. Behold!

(*Hands her a mirror.*)

GALATEA: How beautiful! I'm very glad to know
        That both our tastes agree so perfectly;
        Why, my Pygmalion, I did not think
        That aught could be more beautiful than thou,
        Till I beheld myself. Believe me, love,
        I could look in this mirror all day long.
        So I'm a woman!

PYGMALION: There's no doubt of that!

GALATEA: Oh happy maid to be so passing fair!
        And happier still Pygmalion, who can gaze,
        At will, upon so beautiful a face!

PYGMALION: Hush! Galatea—in thine innocence
        Thou sayest things that others would rebuke.

GALATEA: Indeed, Pygmalion; then it is wrong
        To think that one is exquisitely fair?

PYGMALION: Well, Galatea, it's a sentiment
        That every other woman shares with thee;
        They think it—but they keep it to themselves.

GALATEA: And is thy wife as beautiful as I?

PYGMALION: No, Galatea, for in forming thee
        I took her features—lovely in themselves—
        And in the marble made them lovelier still.

GALATEA (*disappointed*): Oh! then I'm not original

PYGMALION: Well—no—
        That is—thou hast indeed a prototype
        But though in stone thou didst resemble her,
        In life the difference is manifest.

GALATEA: I'm very glad I'm lovelier than she.
        And am I better?

PYGMALION: That I do not know.

GALATEA: Then she has faults?

PYGMALION: But very few indeed;
        Mere trivial blemishes, that serve to show
        That she and I are of one common kin.
        I love her all the better for her faults!

GALATEA (*after a pause*): Tell me some faults and I'll
        commit them now.

PYGMALION: There is no hurry; they will come in time:
        Though for that matter, it's a grievous sin
        To sit as lovingly as we sit now.

GALATEA: Is sin so pleasant? If to sit and talk
        As we are sitting, be indeed a sin,
        Why I could sin all day! But tell me, love,
        Is this great fault that I'm committing now,
        The kind of fault that only serves to show
        That thou and I are of one common kin?

PYGMALION: Indeed, I'm very much afraid it is.

GALATEA: And dost thou love me better for such fault

PYGMALION: Where is the mortal that could answer "no"

GALATEA: Why then I'm satisfied, Pygmalion;
        Thy wife and I can start on equal terms.
        She loves thee?

PYGMALION: Very much.

GALATEA: I'm glad of that.
          I like thy wife.

PYGMALION: And why?

GALATEA: Our tastes agree.
          We love Pygmalion well, and what is more,
          Pygmalion loves us both. I like thy wife;
          I'm sure we shall agree.

PYGMALION (*aside*): I doubt it much!

GALATEA: Is she within?

PYGMALION: No she is not within.

GALATEA: But she'll come back?

PYGMALION: Oh, yes, she will come back.

GALATEA: How pleased she'll be to know when she returns.
          That you are here for us to share.

PYGMALION: (*drily, sarcastically*) Yes, I should say she'd be
          extremely pleased.

GALATEA: Why, there is something in thy voice which says
          That thou art jesting!
          Is it possible
          To say one thing and mean another?

PYGMALION: Yes. It's sometimes done.

GALATEA: How very wonderful;
          So clever!

PYGMALION: And so very useful.

GALATEA: Yes.
          Teach me thy art.

PYGMALION: The art will come in time
          My wife will not be pleased; there—that's the truth

GALATEA: I do not think that I shall like thy wife.
          Tell me more of her. What did she say
          when last she left thee?

PYGMALION: Humph! Well, let me see;
        She wants a child, though true, she gave thee to me—
        As my wife, her solitary representative;
        She feared I should be lonely till she came,
        And counselled me, if thoughts of love should come,
        To speak those thoughts to thee, as I am wont
        To speak to her.

GALATEA: That's right.

PYGMALION: But when she spoke
        Thou wast a stone, now thou art flesh and blood,
        Which makes a difference!

GALATEA: It's a strange world!
        A woman loves her husband very much,
        And cannot brook that I should love him too;
        Lonely she fears he will be lonely too,
        And will not let me cheer your loneliness;
        She bids him breathe his love to senseless stone,
        And when that stone is brought to life—be dumb!
        It's a strange world—I cannot fathom it!

PYGMALION (*aside*): Let me be brave, and put an end to this.
        (*aloud*) Come, Galatea—till my wife returns,
        My sister shall provide thee with a home;
        Her house is close at hand.

GALATEA (*astonished and alarmed*): Send me not hence,
        Pygmalion—let me stay;

PYGMALION: It may not be.
        Come, Galatea, we shall meet again.

GALATEA (*resignedly*): Do with me as thou wilt, Pygmalion!
        But we shall meet again?—and very soon?

PYGMALION: Yes, very soon.

GALATEA: And when thy wife returns,
        She'll let me stay with thee?

PYGMALION: I do not know.

> (*aside*) Why should I bide the truth from her
> (*aloud*) Alas! I may not see thee then.

GALATEA: Pygmalion! What fearful words are these?

PYGMALION: The bitter truth.

> I may not love thee—I must send thee hence.

GALATEA: Recall those words, Pygmalion, my love!

> Was it for this that you have given me life?
> Pygmalion, have mercy on me; see,
> I am thy work, thou hast created me;
> I have been sent to thee. I am thine,
> Thine! only, and unalterably thine!
> This is the thought with which my soul is charged.
> Thou tellest me of one who claims thy love,
> That thou hast love for her alone: Alas I
> do not know these things—I only know
> That I am here to be with thee!
> Thou tellest me of duty to thy wife,
> Of vows that thou wilt love but her; Alas!
> I do not know these things—I only know
> One all-absorbing duty to discharge—
> To love thee, and to make thee love again!

[*During this speech PYGMALION has shown symptoms of irresolution; at its conclusion he takes her in his arms, and embraces her passionately.*]

ACT II

SCENE: SAME AS ACT I

[*PYGMALION discovered at work on an unfinished statue.*]

PYGMALION: To-morrow my Cynisca comes to me;
  Would that she had never departed hence!
  It took a miracle to make me false,
  And even then I was but false in thought;
  A less exacting wife might be appeased
  By that reflection. But Pygmalion
  Must be immaculate in every thought
  Even though Artemis' arms be ranged
  Against the fortress of my constancy!

(*Enter MYRINE, in great excitement.*)

MYRINE: Pygmalion!

PYGMALION: Myrine!

MYRINE: Touch me not,
  Thou hast deceived me, and deceived thy wife!
  Who is the woman thou didst send to me
  To share my roof last night?

PYGMALION: Be pacified;
  Judge neither of us hastily; in truth
  She is as pure, as innocent as thou.

MYRINE: Oh, miserable man—confess the truth!
  Disguise not that of which she boasts aloud!

PYGMALION: Of what then does she boast?

MYRINE: To all I say
  She answers with one parrot-like reply,
  "I love Pygmalion"—and when incensed
  I tell her that thou hast a cheated wife,
  She only says, "I love Pygmalion,
  Who is this shameless woman, sir? Confess!

PYGMALION: Myrine, I will tell thee all. The gods
　　　　　　To punish my expressed impiety,
　　　　　　Have worked a miracle. and brought to life
　　　　　　My statue Galatea!

MYRINE: (*incredulously*). Marvellous,
　　　　　　If it be true!

PYGMALION: It's absolutely true

(*MYRINE opens the curtains and sees the pedeslal empty.*)

MYRINE: The statue's gone! (*GALATEA appears at door.*)

GALATEA: At last we meet! Oh! my Pygmalion!
　　　　　　What strange, strange things have happened since
　　　　　　we met.

PYGMALION: Why, what has happened to thee?

GALATEA: Fearful things!
　　　　　　(*To MYRINE:*) I went with thee into thine house—

MYRINE: Well, well.

GALATEA: And then I sat alone and wept—and wept
　　　　　　A long, long time for my Pygmalion.
　　　　　　Then by degrees, by tedious degrees,
　　　　　　The light—the glorious light!—the god-sent light!
　　　　　　I saw it sink—sink—sink—behind the world!
　　　　　　Then I grew cold—cold—as I used to be.
　　　　　　Before, my loved Pygmalion gave me life.
　　　　　　Then came the fearful thought that, by degrees,
　　　　　　I was returning into stone again!
　　　　　　How bitterly I wept and prayed aloud
　　　　　　That it might not be so! "Spare me, ye gods!
　　　　　　Spare me," I cried, "for my Pygmalion.
　　　　　　"A little longer for Pygmalion!
　　　　　　"Oh, take me not so early from my love;
　　　　　　"Oh, let me see him once—but once again!"

But no—they heard me not, for they are good,
And had they heard, must needs have pitied me;
They had not seen *thee,* and they did not know
The happiness that I must leave behind.
I fell upon thy couch (*to MYRINE*); my eyelids closed;
My senses faded from me one by one
I knew no more until I found myself,
After a strange dark interval of time,
Once more upon my hated pedestal,
A statue—motionless—insensible;
And then I saw the glorious gods come down!
Down to this room! The air was filled with them!
They came and looked upon Pygmalion,
And, looking on him, kissed him one by one,
And said, in tones that spoke to me of life,
"We cannot take her from such happiness!
"Live, Galatea, for his love!" And then
The glorious light that I had lost came back—
There was Myrine's room, there was her couch,
There was the sun in heaven; and the birds
Sang once more in the great green waving trees;
As I had heard them sing—I lived once more
To look on him I love!

MYRINE: Twas but a dream!
Once every day this death occurs to us,
Till thou and I and all who dwell on earth
Shall sleep to wake no more!

GALATEA: To wake no more?

PYGMALION: That time must come—may be not yet awhile—
Still it must come, and we shall all return
To the cold earth from which we quarried thee.

GALATEA: See how the promises of new-born life
Fade from the bright hope-picture, one by one!
Love for Pygmalion, a blighting sin;
His love a shame that he must hide away;

Sleep, stone-like senseless sleep, our natural state;
And life a passing vision born thereof!
How the bright promises fade one by one!

MYRINE: Why there are many men whom thou may'st love;
But not Pygmalion—he has a wife

GALATEA: Does no one love him?

MYRINE: Certainly—I do.
He is my brother.

GALATEA: Did he give thee life?

MYRINE: Why no; but then—

GALATEA: He did not give thee life,
And yet thou lovest him! And why not I
Who owe my very being to his love?

PYGMALION: Well, thou may'st love me—as a father

MYRINE: Yes;
He is thy father, for he gave thee life.

GALATEA: Well, as thou wilt; it is enough to know
That I may love thee. Wilt thou love me too?

PYGMALION: Yes, as a daughter; there, that's understood.

GALATEA: Then I am satisfied.

MYRINE: (aside) Indeed I hope
Cynisca also will be satisfied! (*exit MYRINE*)

GALATEA (*to PYGMALION*): Thou art not going from me?

PYGMALION: For a while.

GALATEA: Oh, take me with thee; leave me not alone
With these cold emblems of my former self!
(*alluding to statues*) I dare not look at them!

PYGMALION: Leucippe comes,
And he shall comfort thee until I return;
I'll not be long!

GALATEA: Leucippe! Who's he?

PYGMALION: A valiant soldier.

GALATEA: What is that?

PYGMALION: A man,
         Who's hired to kill his country's enemies.

GALATEA (*horrified*): A paid assassin!

PYGMALION (*annoyed*): Well that's rather strong.
         There spoke the thoroughly untutored mind;
         So coarse a sentiment might fairly pass
         With mere Arcadians—a cultured state
         Holds soldiers at a higher estimate.
         In Athens—which is highly civilized—
         The soldier's social rank is in itself
         Almost a patent of nobility.

GALATEA: He Kills! And he is paid to kill!

PYGMALION: No doubt.
         But then he kills to save his countrymen.

GALATEA: Whether his countrymen be right or wrong?

PYGMALION: He don't go into that—it's quite enough
         That there are enemies for him to kill;
         He goes and kills them when his orders come

GALATEA: How terrible! Why, my Pygmalion,
         How many dreadful things thou teachest me
         Thou tellest me of death—that hideous doom
         That all must fill; and having told me this
         Here is a man, whose business is to kill
         To filch from other men the priceless boon
         That thou hast given me—the boon of life—
         And thou defendest him!

PYGMALION: I have no time
         To make these matters—here he comes;
         Talk to him—thou wilt find him kind and good,
         Despite his terrible profession.

GALATEA (*in great terror*): No!
        I'll not be left with him, Pygmalion. Stay!
        He is a murderer!

PYGMALION: Ridiculous!
        Why, Galatea, he will harm thee not
        He is as good as brave. I'll not be long,
        I'll soon return. Farewell!

GALATEA: I will obey
        Since thou desirest it; but to be left
        Alone with one whose mission is to kill!
        Oh, it is terrible!

(*Enter LEUCIPPE with a Fawn that he has shot.*)

LEUCIPPE: A splendid shot,
        And one that I shall never make again!

GALATEA: Monster! Approach me not!
        (*Shrinking into corner.*)

LEUCIPPE: Why, who is this?
        Nay, I'll not hurt thee, maiden!

GALATEA: Spare me, sir
        I have not done thy country any wrong!
        I am no enemy!

LEUCIPPE: I'll swear to that
        Were Athens' enemies as fair as thou,
        She'd never be at loss for warriors.

GALATEA: Oh miserable man, repent! Repent!
        Ere the stern marble claim you once again.

LEUCIPPE: I don't quite understand—

GALATEA: Remember, sir,
        The sculptor who designed you, little thought
        That when he prayed the gods to give you life,
        He turned a monster loose upon the world!

        See, there is blood upon those cruel hands!
        Oh touch me not!

LEUCIPPE (*aside*): Poor crazy little girl!
        Why—there's no cause for fear—I'll harm thee not—
        As for the blood, this will account for it (*showing*
        Fawn).

GALATEA: What's that?

LEUCIPPE: A little Fawn.

GALATEA: It does not move!

LEUCIPPE: No, for I wounded her.

GALATEA: Oh, horrible!

LEUCIPPE: Poor little thing! 'Twas almost accident;
        I lay upon my back beneath a tree,
        Whistling the lazy hours away—when lo!
        I saw her bounding through a distant glade;
        My bow was handy; in sheer wantonness
        I aimed an arrow at her, and let fly,
        Believing that at near a hundred yards
        So small a being would be safe enough,
        But, strange to tell, I hit her. Here she is
        She moves—poor little lady! Ah, she's dead!

GALATEA: Oh, horrible! oh, miserable man!
        What have you done*? (Takes Fawn into her arms*)
        Why, you have murdered her!
        Poor little thing! I know not what thou art;
        Thy form is strange to me; but thou hadst life
        And he has robbed thee of it! (*Gives it back to*
        LEUCIPPE)
        Get you hence!
        Ere vengeance overtake you!

LEUCIPPE: Well, in truth,
        I have some apprehension on that score.
        It was Myrine's—though I knew it not!

'Twould pain her much to know that it is dead;
So keep the matter carefully from her
Until I can replace it. (*Exit Leucippe with Fawn*)

GALATEA: Get you hence;
I have no compact with a murderer!

(*Enter MYRINE*)

MYRINE: Why, Galatea, what has frightened thee?

GALATEA: Myrine, I have that to say to thee
That thou must nerve thyself to hear. That man—
The man thou lovest—is a murderer!

MYRINE: Poor little maid! Pygmalion, ere he left,
Told me that by that name thou didst describe
The bravest soldier that our country owns!
He's no assassin, he's a warrior.

GALATEA: Then what is an assassin?

MYRINE: One who wars
Only with weak, defenceless creatures. One
Whose calling is to murder unawares.
My brave Leucippe is no murderer.

GALATEA: Thy brave Leucippe is no longer brave,
He is a mere assassin by thy showing.
I saw him with his victim in his arms,
His wicked hands dyed crimson with her blood!
There she lay, cold and stark—her gentle eyes
Glazed with the film of death. She moved but once,
She turned her head to him and tried to speak,
But ere she could articulate a word
Her head fell helplessly, and she was dead!

MYRINE: Why, you are raving, girl! Who told you this?

GALATEA: He owned it; and he gloried in the deed.
He told me how, in arrant wantonness,
He drew his bow, and smote her to the heart!

MYRINE: Leucippe did all this! Impossible?
            You must be dreaming!

GALATEA: On my life, it's true.
            See, here's a handkerchief which still is stained
            With her life-blood—I staunched it with my hand.

MYRINE: Who was his victim?

GALATEA: Nay—I cannot tell.
            Her form was strange to me—but here he comes;
            Oh, hide me from that wicked murderer!

                     (*Enter LEUCIPPE*)

MYRINE: Leucippe, can this dreadful tale be true?

LEUCIPPE (*to GALATEA, aside*): Thou should have kept my secret.
            See, poor girl,
            How it distresses her. (*to MYRINE*) It's true enough,
            But Galatea should have kept it close,
            I knew that it would pain thee grievously.

MYRINE: Some devil must have turned Leucippe's brain!
            You did all this?

LEUCIPPE: Undoubtedly I did.
            I saw my victim dancing happily
            Across my field of view—I took my bow,
            And, at the distance of a hundred yards,
            I sent an arrow right into her heart.
            There are few soldiers who could do as much.

MYRINE: Indeed I hope that there are very few.
            Oh, miserable man!

LEUCIPPE: That's rather hard.
            Congratulate me rather on my aim,
            Of which I have some reason now to boast;
            As for my victim—why, one more or less,
            What does it matter? There are plenty left!
            And then reflect—indeed, I never thought

That I should hit her at so long a range;
My aim was truer than I thought it was,
And the poor little lady's dead!

MYRINE: Alas!
This is the calmness of insanity.
What shall we do? Go, hide yourself away—

LEUCIPPE: But—

MYRINE: Not a word—I will not hear thy voice,
I will not look upon thy face again;
Begone!

GALATEA: Go, sir, or I'll alarm the house!

LEUCIPPE: Well, this is sensibility, indeed!
Well, they are women—women judge these thingsl
By some disjointed logic of their own,
That is not given to man to understand.
I'm off to Athens—when your reason comes
Send for me, if you will. Till then, farewell.
(*Exit angrily*)

MYRINE: Oh, this must be a dream, and I shall wake
To happiness once more!

GALATEA: A dream! no doubt!
We both are dreaming, and we dream the same!
But by what sign, Myrine, can we tell
Whether we dream or wake?

MYRINE: There are some things
Too terrible for truth, and this is one.

(*Enter PYGMALION, with Fawn*)

PYGMALION: Why, what's the matter with Leucippe, girl?
I saw him leave the house, and mount his horse
With every show of anger.

MYRINE: He is mad,
        And he hath done a deed I dare not name.
        Did he say ought to thee before he left?

PYGMALION: Yes, when I asked him what had angered him
        He threw me this (*showing Fawn*).

GALATEA (*in extreme of horror*): His victim! take it hence!
        I cannot look at it!

MYRINE: Why what is this?

GALATEA: The being he destroyed in wantonness;
        He robbed it of the life the gods had given.
        Oh! take it hence I dare not look on death!

MYRINE: Why, was this all he killed?

GALATEA (*astonished*): All!!! And enough!

MYRINE: Why, girl—thou must be mad! Pygmalion—
        She told me he had murdered somebody,
        But knew not whom!

PYGMALION: The girl will drive us mad
        Bid them prepare my horse—I'll bring him back

(*Exit MYRINE*)

GALATEA: Have I done wrong? Indeed, I did not know:
        Thou art angry with me?

PYGMALION: Yes, I am;
        I'm more than angry with thee—not content
        With publishing thine unmasked love for me,
        Thou hast estranged Leucippe from his love
        Through thine unwarrantable foolishness.

(*Enter MIMOS*)

MIMOS: Sir, Chrysos and his lady are without.

PYGMALION: I cannot see them now. Stay—show them in.
        (*Exit MIMOS; to GALATEA*) Go, wait in there. I'll
        join thee very soon.

(Exit GALATEA)
(Enter DAPHNE)

DAPHNE: Where is Pygmalion?

PYGMALION: Pygmalion's here.

DAPHNE: We called upon you many months ago,
But you were not at home—so being here,
We looked around us and we saw the stone
You keep so carefully behind that veil.

PYGMALION: That was a most outrageous liberty.

DAPHNE: Sir! Do you know me?

PYGMALION: You are Chrysos', wife.
Has Chrysos come with you?

DAPHNE: He waits without.
I am his herald to prepare you for
The honour he confers. Be civil, sir,
And he may buy that statue; if he does
Your fortune's made!

PYGMALION (*to MIMOS*): You'd better send him in.

(Exit MIMOS)
(Enter CHRYSOS)

CHRYSOS: Well—is the young man's mind prepared?

DAPHNE: It is;
He seems quite calm. Give money for the stone.
I've heard that it is far beyond all price,
But run it down; abuse it ere you buy.

CHRYSOS (*to PYGMALION*): Where is the statue that I saw last year?

PYGMALION: Sir—it's unfinished—it's a clumsy thing.
I am ashamed of it.

CHRYSOS: It isn't good.
There's want of depth; it's much too hard and thin;
Then the half distances are very crude—
Oh—very crude indeed—then it lacks air,

And wind and motion, massive light and shade;
It's very roughly chiseled; on my soul
The carving's damnable!

DAPHNE (*aside to him*): Bethink—yourself
That's said of painting—this is sculpture!

CHRYSOS: Eh?
It's the same thing, the principle's the same;
Now for its price. Let's, see—what will it weigh?

DAPHNE: A ton, or thereabouts.

CHRYSOS: Suppose we say
A thousand drachmas?

PYGMALION: No no, no, my lord!
The work is very crude and thin, and then
Remember, sir, the modeling—

CHRYSOS: Damnable!
But never mind, although the thing is poor,
'Twill serve to hold a candle in my hall.

PYGMALION: Excuse me, sir; poor though that statue be,
I value it beyond all price.

CHRYSOS: Pooh, pooh!
I give a thousand drachmas for a stone
Which in the rough would not fetch half that sum!

DAPHNE: Why bless my soul, young man, are you aware
We gave but fifteen hundred not long since
For an Apollo twice as big as that?

PYGMALION: But pardon me, a sculptor does not test
The beauty of a figure by its bulk.

CHRYSOS: Ah! then she does.

DAPHNE: Young man, you'd best take care,
You are offending Chrysos! (*Exit*)

CHRYSOS: And his wife. (*going*)

PYGMALION: I cannot stay to enter into that
        Sir, once for all, the statue's not for sale. (*Exit*)

CHRYSOS: Sir, once for all, I will not be denied;
        Confound it—if a patron of the arts
        Is thus to be dictated to by art,
        What comes of that art patron's patronage?
        He must be taught a lesson—where's the stone?
        (*Goes to pedestal and opens the curtains*)
        It's gone! (*Enter GALATEA, he stares at her in astonishment.*) Hallo! What's this?

GALATEA: Are you unwell?

CHRYSOS: *Oh, no*—I fancied just at first—pooh, pooh!
        Ridiculous. (*Aside*). And yet it's very like!
        (*Aloud*). I know your face, have'nt I seen you in—
        In—in (*puzzling himself*).

GALATEA: In marble? Very probably.

CHRYSOS: Oh, now I understand. Why this must be
        Pygmalion's model! Yes, of course it is.
        A very bold-faced woman, I'll be bound.
        These models always are. I'll speak with her.
        Come hither, maiden.

GALATEA (*who has been examining him in great wonder*):
        Tell, me, what *are* you?

CHRYSOS: What *am* I?

GALATEA: Yes, I mean, are you a man?

CHRYSOS: Well, yes; I'm told so.

GALATEA: Then believe them not,
        They've been deceiving you.

CHRYSOS: The deuce they have!

GALATEA: A man is very tall, and straight, and strong,
        With big brave eyes, fair face, and tender voice.
        I've seen one.

CHRYSOS: *Have* you?

GALATEA: Yes, you are no man.

CHRYSOS: Does the young person take me for a woman?

GALATEA: A woman? No; a woman's soft and weak,
    And fair, and exquisitely beautiful.
    I am a woman; you are not like me.

CHRYSOS: Nature forbid that I should be like you,
    And sow my features at so much an hour!

GALATEA: And yet I like you, for you make me laugh;
    You are so round and red, your eyes so small,
    Your mouth so large, your face so seared with lines,
    And then you are so little and so fat!

CHRYSOS (*aside*): This is a most extraordinary girl.

GALATEA: Oh, stay—I understand—Pygmalion's skill
    Is the result of long experience.
    The individual who modelled you
    Was a beginner very probably?

CHRYSOS (*puzzled*): No. I have seven elder brothers.
    Strange
    That one so young should be so very bold

GALATEA: This is not boldness, it is innocence
    Pygmalion says so, and he ought to know.

CHRYSOS: No doubt, but I was not born yesterday. (*Sits.*)

GALATEA: Indeed!—I was (*He beckons her to sit beside him*)
    How awkwardly you sit.

CHRYSOS: I'm not aware that there is anything
    Extraordinary in my sitting down
    The nature of the seated attitude
    Does not leave scope for much variety.

GALATEA: I never saw Pygmalion sit like that.

CHRYSOS: Doesn't he sit down like other men?

GALATEA: Of course!
          He always puts his arm around my waist.

CHRYSOS: The deuce he does! Artistic reprobate!

GALATEA: But you do not. Perhaps you don't know how?

CHRYSOS: Oh yes I *do* know how!

GALATEA: Well, do it then!

CHRYSOS: It's a strange whim but I will humour her
          You're sure it's innocence? (*Does so*)

GALATEA: Of course it is!
          I tell you I was born but yesterday.

CHRYSOS: Who is your mother?

GALATEA: I never had one. I'm Pygmalion's child;
          Have people usually mothers?

CHRYSOS: Well, That is the rule.

GALATEA: But then Pygmalion
          Is cleverer than most men.

CHRYSOS: Yes, I've heard
          That he has powers denied to other men,
          And I'm beginning to believe it!

(*Enter DAPHNE*)

DAPHNE: Why, What's this?

(*CHRYSOS quickly moves away from GALATEA*)

CHRYSOS: My wife!

DAPHNE: Can I believe my eyes (*GALATEA rises*)

CHRYSOS: No!

DAPHNE: *Who's* this woman? Why, how very like—

CHRYSOS: Like what?

DAPHNE: That statue that we wished to buy—
          The self-same face, the self-same drapery,

In every detail it's identical.
Why, one would almost think Pygmalion,
By some strange means, had brought the thing to life;
So marvellous her likeness to that stone!

CHRYSOS (*aside*): A very good idea, and one that I
May well improve upon. It's rather rash,
But desperate ills need desperate remedies.
Now for a good one. Daphne, calm yourself.
You know the statue that we spoke of? Well
The gods have worked a miracle on it
And it has come to life. Behold it here!

DAPHNE: Bah! Do you think me mad?

GALATEA: His tale is true—
I was a cold unfeeling block of stone
Inanimate—insensible—until
Pygmalion, by the ardour of his prayers,
Kindled the spark of life within my frame,
And made me what I am!

CHRYSOS (*aside to GALATEA*): That's very good;
Go on and keep it up.

DAPHNE: You brazen girl,
I am his wife!

GALATEA: His wife? (To Chrysos.) Then get you hence,
I may not love you when your wife is here.

DAPHNE: Why, what unknown audacity is this?

CHRYSOS: It's the audacity of innocence;
Don't judge her by the rules that govern you,
She was born yesterday, and you were not!
(*Enter MIMOS*)

MIMOS: My lord, Pygmalion's here.

CHRYSOS (*aside*): He'll ruin all.

DAPHNE (*to MIMOS*): Who is this woman?

CHRYSOS: Why, I've told you, she—

DAPHNE: Stop, not a word! I'll have it from *his* lips!

GALATEA: Why ask him when I tell you—?

DAPHNE: Hold your tongue!
        (*to MIMOS*) Who is this woman? If you tell a lie
        I'll have you whipped.

MIMOS: Oh, I shall tell no lie!
        That is a statue that has come to life.

CHRYSOS (*aside to MIMOS*): I'm very much obliged to you!
        (*Gives him money*)
        (*Enter MYRINE*)

MYRINE: What's this?
        Is anything the matter?

DAPHNE: Certainly.
        This woman—

MYRINE: Is a statue come to life.

CHRYSOS: I'm very much obliged to you!
        (*Enter PYGMALION*)

PYGMALION: How now
        Chrysos?

CHRYSOS: The statue!—

DAPHNE: Stop!

CHRYSOS: Let me explain.
        The statue that I purchased—

DAPHNE: Let me speak.
        Chrysos—this girl, Myrine, and your slave,
        Have all agreed to tell me she is—

PYGMALION: The statue, Galatea, come to life?
        Undoubtedly she is!

CHRYSOS: It seems to me,
        I'm very much obliged to every one!

(*Enter CYNISCA*)

CYNISCA: Pygmalion, my love!

PYGMALION: Cynisca here!

CYNISCA: And even earlier than hoped to be.
>(*aside*) Why, who are these? (*aloud*) I beg your
>pardon, sir,
>I thought my husband was alone.

DAPHNE (*maliciously*): No doubt.
>I also thought my husband alone:
>We wives are too believing.

CYNISCA (*aside to PYGMALION*): Who are these?

PYGMALION: Why, this. is Chrysos, this is Daphne. They
>Have come—

DAPHNE: On very different errands, sir.
>Chrysos has come to see this brazen girl;
>I have come after Chrysos—

CHRYSOS: As you keep
>So strictly to the sequence of events
>Add this—Pygmalion came after *you*!

CYNISCA: Who is this lady (*alluding to GALATEA*)? Why,
>Impossible!

DAPHNE: Oh, not at all!

CYNISCA (*turning to pedestal*): And yet the statue's gone!

PYGMALION: Cynisca, miracles have taken place;
>The gods have given Galatea life!

CYNISCA: Oh, marvellous! Is this indeed the form
>That my Pygmalion fashioned with his hands?

PYGMALION: . Indeed it is.

CYNISCA: Why, let me look at her!
>Yes it's the same fair face—the same fair form;
>Clad in the same fair folds of drapery!

GALATEA: And dost thou know me then?

CYNISCA: Hear her! she speaks!
> Our Galatea speaks aloud! Know thee?
> Why I have sat for hours, and watched thee grow;
> Sat—motionless as thou—wrapped in his work,
> Save only that in very ecstasy
> I hurried ever and anon to kiss
> The glorious hands that made thee all thou art!
> Come—let me kiss thee with a mother's love
> (*kisses her*)
> See she can kiss!

DAPHNE: Yes, I'll be bound she can!

CYNISCA: Why my Pygmalion, where is the joy
> That ought to animate that face of thine,
> Now that the gods have crowned thy wondrous
> skill?

CHRYSOS (*aside to PYGMALION*): Stick to our story;
> bold-faced though she be,
> She's very young, and may perhaps repent
> It's terrible to have to tell a lie,
> But if it must be told—why, tell it well!

CYNISCA: I see it all. I have returned too soon.

DAPHNE: No, I'm afraid you have returned too late;
> Cynisca, never leave that man again,
> Or leave him altogether!

CYNISCA (*astonished*): Why, what's this?

GALATEA: Oh, madam, bear with him, and blame him not
> Judge him not hastily; in every word,
> In every thought he has obeyed thy wish.
> Thou badst him speak to me as unto thee;
> And he and I have sat as lovingly
> As if thou hadst been present to behold
> How faithfully thy wishes were obeyed!

CYNISCA: Pygmalion! What is this?

PYGMALION: Go, get thee hence;
    Thou shouldst not see the fearful consequence
    That must attend those heedless words of thine!

GALATEA: Judge him not hastily, he's not like this
    When he and I are sitting here alone.
    He has two voices, and two faces madam,
    One for the world, and one for him and me!

CYNISCA: Thy wife against thine eyes! those are the
    stakes!
    Well thou hast played thy game, and thou has lost!

PYGMALION: Cynisca, hear me! In a cursed hour
    I prayed for power to give that statue life.
    My impious prayer aroused the outraged gods,
    They are my judges, leave me in their hands;
    I have been false to them, but not to thee!
    Spare me!

CYNISCA: Oh, pitiful adventurer!
    He dares to lose, but does not dare to pay!
    Come, be a man! See, I am brave enough
    And I have more to bear than thou! Behold!
    I am alone, thou hast thy statue bride!
    Oh, Artemis, my mistress, bear me—now,
    Ere I remember how I love that man,
    And in that memory forget my shame!
    If he in deed or thought hath been untrue,
    Be just and let him pay the penalty!

    (*PYGMALION, with an exclamation,*
    covers his eyes with his hands.)

GALATEA: Cynisca, pity him!

CYNISCA: I know no pity, woman; for the act
That thawed thee into flesh has hardened me
Into the cursed stone from which thou cam'st.
We have changed places; from this moment forth
Be *thou* the wife and I the senseless stone!

(*Thrusts GALATEA from her.*)

ACT III

SCENE: SAME AS ACTS I AND II

(Enter DAPHNE)

DAPHNE: It seems Pygmalion has the awesome gift
Of bringing, stone to life. I'll question him
And ascertain how far that power extends
(Enter MYRINE, weeping)
Myrine—and in tears! Why, what's amiss

MYRINE: Oh we were all so happy yesterday,
And now, within twelve miserable hours,
A blight has fallen upon all of us.
Pygmalion is blind as death itself,
Cynisca leaves his home this very day,
And my Leucippe hath deserted me!
I shall go mad with all this weight of grief!

DAPHNE: All this is Galatea's work?

MYRINE: Yes, all.

DAPHNE: But can't you stop her? Shut the creature up
Dispose of her, or break her? Won't she chip?

MYRINE: No, I'm afraid not.

DAPHNE: Ah, were I his wife
I'd spoil her beauty! There'd be little chance
Of finding him and her alone again!

MYRINE: There's little need to take precautions now
For he, alas! is blind.

DAPHNE: Blind! What of that?
Man has five senses; if he loses one
The vital energy on which it fed
Goes to intensify the other four.
He had five arrows in his quiver; well,

He has shot one away, and four remain.
My dear, an enemy is not disarmed
Because he's lost one arrow out of five!

MYRINE: The punishment he undergoes might well content
his wife!

DAPHNE: A happy woman, that!

MYRINE: Cynisca happy?

DAPHNE To be sure she is;
She has the power to punish faithlessness,
And she has used it on her faithless spouse.
Had I Cynisca's privilege, I swear
I'd never let my Chrysos rest in peace,
Until he warranted my using it!
Pygmalion's wronged her, and she's punished him.
What more could woman want?
(Enter CYNISCA)

CYNISCA: What more? Why, this!
The power to tame my tongue to speak the words
That would restore him to his former self!
The power to quell the fierce, unruly soul
That battles with my miserable heart!
The power to say, "Oh, my Pygmalion,
"My love is thine to hold or cast away,
"Do with it as thou wilt; it cannot die!"
I'd barter half my miserable life
For power to say these few true words to him!

MYRINE: Why, then there's hope for him?

CYNISCA: There's none indeed!
This day I'll leave his home and hide away
Where I can brood upon my shame. I'll fan
The smouldering fire of jealousy until
It bursts into an all-devouring flame,
And pray that I may perish in its glow!

DAPHNE: That's bravely said, Cynisca! Never fear;
     Pygmalion will give thee wherewithal
     To nurture it.

CYNISCA (*passionately*): I need not wherewithal!
     I carry wherewithal within my heart!
     Oh, I can conjure up the scene at will
     When he and she sit lovingly alone.
     I know too well the devilish art he works,
     And how his guilty passion shapes itself.
     I follow him through every twist and turn
     By which he wormed himself into my heart;
     I hear him breathing to the guilty girl
     The fond familiar nothings of our love;
     I hear him whispering into *her* ear
     The tenderness that he rehearsed on me.
     I follow him through all his well-known moods
     Now fierce and passionate, now fanciful;
     And ever tuning his accursed tongue
     To chime in with the passion at her heart:
     Oh, never fear that I shall starve the flame!
     When jealousy takes shelter in *my* heart,
     It does not die for lack of sustenance!

DAPHNE: Come to my home, and thou shall feed it there;
     We'll play at widows, and we'll pass our time
     Railing against the perfidy of man.

CYNISCA: But Chrysos?—

DAPHNE: Chrysos? Oh, you won't see him.

CYNISCA: How so?

DAPHNE: How so? I've turned him out of doors!
     Why, does the girl consider jealousy
     Her unassailable prerogative?
     Thou hast thy vengeance on Pygmalion
     He can no longer feast upon *thy* face.

Well, Chrysos can no longer feast on mine!
I can't put out his eyes (I wish I could!)
But I can shut them out, and that I've done.

CYNISCA: I thank you, madam, and I'll go with you

MYRINE: No no; thou shalt not leave Pygmalion;
He will not live if thou desertest him.
Add nothing to his pain—this second blow
Might well complete the work thou hast begun!

CYNISCA: Nay, let me go—I must not see his face;
For if I look on him I may relent.
Detain me not, Myrine—fare thee well

(*Exit CYNSICA, MYRINE follows her*)

DAPHNE: Well, there'll be pretty scenes in Athens now

(*CHRYSOS enters unobserved.*)

Why, I have daughters—all of them of age—
What chance is there for plain young women, now
That every man may take a block of stone
And carve a family to suit his tastes?

CHRYSOS: If every woman were a Daphne, man
Would never care to look on sculptured stone!
Oh, Daphne!

DAPHNE: Monster—get you hence, away!
I'll hold no converse with you, get you gone.
(*Aside*) If I'd Cynisca's tongue I'd wither him!
(*Imitating CYNISCA*) "Oh, I can conjure up the
scene at *will*
"Where you and she sit lovingly alone!
"Oh, never fear that I will starve the flame:
"When jealousy takes shelter in my heart,
"It does not die for lack of sustenance!"

CHRYSOS: I'm sure of that! your hospitality
                Is world-renowned. Extend it, love, to me!
                Oh. take me home again!

DAPHNE: Home? no, not I!
                Why I've a Gallery of goddesses,
                Fifty at least—half-dressed bacchantes, too—
                Dryads and water-nymphs of every kind;
                Suppose I find, when I go home to-day,
                That they've all taken it into their heads
                To come to life—what would become of them,
                Or me, with Chrysos in the house? No-no,
                They're bad enough in marble—but in flesh!!!
                I'll sell the bold-faced hussies one and all,
                But till I've sold them, Chrysos stays outside!

CHRYSOS: What have I done?

DAPHNE: What have you not done sir?

CHRYSOS: I cannot tell you—it would take too long!

DAPHNE: I saw you sitting with that marble minx,
                Your arm pressed lovingly around her waist
                Explain that Chrysos.

CHRYSOS: It explains itself:
                I am a zealous patron of the arts,
                And I am very fond of statuary.

DAPHNE: Bah—I've artistic tastes as well as you
                But still, you never saw me sitting with
                My arms around a stone Apollo's waist!
                As for this "statue"—could I see her now,
                I'd test your taste for fragments!

CHRYSOS: Spare the girl,
                She's very young and very innocent
                She claims your pity

DAPHNE: Does she?

CHRYSOS: Yes, she does
            If I saw Daphne sitting with her arm
            Round an Apollo, I should slay him.

DAPHNE (*relenting*): Would you?

CHRYSOS: I should upon my word, I should

DAPHNE: Well, Chrysos, thou art pardoned. After all
            The circumstances were exceptional.

CHRYSOS (*aside*): Unhappily, they were!

DAPHNE: Come home, but mind
            I'll sell my gallery of goddesses;
            No good can come of animating stone.

CHRYSOS: Oh, pardon me—why every soul on earth
            Sprang from the stones Deucalion threw behind

DAPHNE: But Deucalion only *threw* the stones
            He left it to the gods to fashion them

CHRYSOS (*aside, looking at her*): And we who've seen
            the work the gods turn out,
            Would rather leave it to Pygmalion!

DAPHNE (*taking CHRYSOS' arm, who is looking at a statue of Venus*): Come along, do! (*Exit*)

(*Enter MYRINE, in great distresss*)

MYRINE: Pygmalion's heard that he must lose his wife,
            And swears by all the gods that reign above
            He will not live if she deserts him now!
            What-what is to be done?

(*Enter GALATEA*)

GALATEA: Myrine here!
            Where is Pygmalion?

MYRINE: Oh, wretched girl!
            Art thou not satisfied with all the ill
            Thy heedlessness has worked that thou art come

> To gaze upon thy victim's misery?
> Well, thou hast come in time!

GALATEA: What dost thou mean?

MYRINE: Why this is what I mean—he will not live
> Now that Cynisca has deserted him.
> Oh, girl, his blood will be upon thy head!

GALATEA: Pygmalion will not live! Pygmalion die!
> And I, alas, the miserable cause!
> Oh, what is to be done?

MYRINE: I do not know.
> And yet there is one chance, but one alone;
> I'll see Cynisca, and prevail on her
> To meet Pygmalion but once again.

GALATEA (*Wildly*): But should she come too late?
> he may not live
> Till she returns.

MYRINE: I'll send him now to thee,
> And tell him that his wife awaits him here.
> He'll take thee for Cynisca; when he speaks
> Answer thou him as if thou wast his wife.

GALATEA: Yes, yes, I understand.

MYRINE: Then I'll begone,
> The gods assist thee in this artifice! (*Exit MYRINE*)

GALATEA: The gods will help me, for the gods are good.
> Oh, Heaven, in this great grief I turn to thee.
> Teach me to speak to him, as, ere I lived,
> Cynisca spake to him. Oh, let my voice
> Be to Pygmalion as Cynisca's voice,
> And he will live—for her and not for me—
> Yet he will live. I am the fountain head

(Enter PYGMALION, unobserved, led by MYRINE)

Of all the horrors that surround him now;
And it is fit that I should suffer this;
Grant this, my first appeal—I do not ask
Pygmalion's love; I ask Pygmalion's life!

(*PYGMALION utters an exclamation of joy. She rushes to
him and seizes his hand.*)

Pygmalion!

PYGMALION: I have no words in which
                    To tell the joy with which I heard that prayer.
                    Oh, take me to thine arms, my dearly loved!
                    And teach me once again how much I risked
                    In risking such a heaven-sent love as thine.

GALATEA (*believing that he refers to her*): Pygmalion!
                    my love! Pygmalion!
                    Once more those words! again! say them again!
                    Tell me that thou forgivest me the ill
                    That I unwittingly have worked on thee!

PYGMALION: Forgive *thee?* Why, my wife, I did not dare
                    To ask thy pardon, and thou askest mine.
                    The compact with thy mistress Artemis
                    Gave thee a heaven-sent right to punish me,
                    I've learnt to take whate'er the gods may send.

(*GALATEA, at first delighted, learns in the course of this
speech that PYGMALION takes her for CYNISCA, and
expresses extreme anguish*)

GALATEA (*with an effort*): But then, this woman, Galatea—
PYGMALION: Well?
GALATEA: Thy love for her is dead?
PYGMALION: I had no love.
GALATEA: Thou hadst no love?

PYGMALION: No love. At first, in truth,
        In mad amazement at the miracle
        That crowned my handiwork, and brought to life
        The fair creation of my sculptor's skill,
        I yielded to her god-sent influence, For I had wor-
        shipped her before she lived
        Because she called Cynisca's face to me;
        But when she lived—that love died, word by word.

GALATEA: That is well said; thou dost not love her then?
        She is no more to thee than senseless stone?

PYGMALION: Speak not of her, Cynisca, for I swear

        (*Enter CYNISCA, unobserved*)

        The unhewn marble of Pentelicus
        Hath charms for me, which she, in all her glow
        Of womanly perfection, could not match.

GALATEA: I'm very glad to hear that this is so.
        Thou art forgiven! (*Kisses his forehead*)

PYGMALION: Thou hast pardoned me,
        And though the law of Artemis declared
        Thy pardon should restore to me the light
        Thine anger took away, I would be blind,
        I would not have mine eyes lest they should rest
        On her who caused me all this bitterness!

GALATEA: Indeed, Pygmalion—'twere better thus
        If thou could'st look on Galatea now,
        Thy love for her, perchance, might come again!

PYGMALION: No, no.

GALATEA: They say that she endureth pains
        That mock the power of words!

PYGMALION: It should be so!

GALATEA: Hast thou *no* pity for her?

PYGMALION: No, not I.
    The ill that she hath worked on thee—on me—
    And on Myrine—surely were enough
    To make us curse the hour that gave her life.
    She is not fit to live upon this world!

GALATEA (*bitterly*): Upon this worthy world, thou sayest well,
    The woman shall be seen of thee no more.

(Takes CYNISCA's hand and leads her to PYGMALION)

    What would'st thou with her now?
    Thou hast *thy wife!*

(She substitutes CYNISCA, and retires, weeping. CYNISCA takes him to her arms and kisses him. He recovers his sight)

PYGMALION: Cynisca! See! the light of day is mine!
    Once more I look upon thy well-loved face!

(Enter MYRINE, and LEUCIPPE)

LEUCIPPE: Pygmalion! Thou hast thine eyes again!
    Come—this is happiness indeed!

PYGMALION: And thou!
    Myrine has recalled thee?

LEUCIPPE: No, I came,
    But more in sorrow than in penitence;
    For I've a hardened and a blood-stained heart!
    I thought she would denounce me to the law,
    But time, I found, had worked a wondrous change;
    The very girl, who half-a-day ago
    Had cursed me for a ruthless murderer,
    Not only pardoned me my infamy,
    But absolutely hugged me with delight,
    When she, with hungry and unpitying eyes,
    Beheld my victim—at the kitchen fire!
    The little cannibal!

(Enter GALATEA)

PYGMALION: Away from me,
                    Woman or statue! Thou the only blight
                    That ever fell upon my love—begone,
                    For thou hast been the curse of all who fell
                    Within the compass of thy waywardness!

CYNISCA: No, no—recall those words Pygmalion,
                    Thou knowest not all.

GALATEA: Nay—let me go from him;
                    That *curse—his curse—still* ringing in mine ears,
                    For life is bitterer to me than death.

                    (She mounts the steps of pedestal.)

                    Farewell, Pygmalion! Farewell! Farewell!

                    (*The curtains conceal her.*)

CYNISCA: Thou art unjust to her as I to thee!
                    Her's was the voice that pardoned thee—not mine.
                    I knew no pity till she taught it me.
                    I heard the words she spoke, and little thought
                    That they would find an echo in my heart;
                    But so it was. I took them for mine own,
                    And asking for thy pardon, pardoned thee!

PYGMALION (*amazed*): Cynisca! Is this so?

CYNISCA: In truth it is!

GALATEA (*behind curtain*): Farewell, Pygmalion! Farewell!
                    Cynisca! Farewell!

*(PYGMALION rushes to the veil and tears it away, discovering
GALATEA as a statue on the pedestal, as in Act I.)*

THE END

[*or continue on the following page for a second ending.*]

LIGHTS OUT.

(Cast takes bows . . . GALATEA remaining on her pedestal)

CYNISCA *(approaches audience)*: This ending's not to my
                 delight. My womb *(turns to PYGMALION)*
                 Still bare, you reproduce, with cunning art,
                 One hundred thousand fold. The victory,
                 The fame, the fortune yours, while Demeter
                 Denied my prayer.

PYGMALION: My dear, my muse, my love,
                 You brought to life these stones around us. Yours
                 The image made like life, becoming life.

CYNISCA: But only Gods make life, you said to me.
                 Galatea's cold, dull stone again.
                 I sat for months, her model,while you carved
                 her from me. Our daughter she should be.
                 (She enters the audience space.)
                 You have helped bring this play to life.
                 Now you, our faithful ones, come forth and bring
                 My copy—who was born yesterday—
                 Back to life. Play your part that I
                 May have my wish. Who among you, God-like,
                 Will bring her back to life?

(CYNISCA improvises with audience members to serve as co-creators of GALATEA's rebirth. GALATEA takes her place at CYNISCA's knee with PYGMALION, his slave MIMOS close by. They all—including audience member—take a final bow.)

LIGHTS DIM

THE END

[Some such ending would facilitate a theater's post-production discussion of the play. Otherwise the play ends on the previous page.]

Chapter Two
Reproducing Gender Roles
in Victorian England
Carolyn Williams, Ph.D.

The Victorian period is known for its norms, roles, and expectations having to do with gender. In historical retrospect, we can very clearly see that modern gender arrangements were established gradually, taking fixed shape in the late eighteenth and early nineteenth centuries. Before that, both men and women participated in the economic life of the family (McKeon, 1995). The rise of Gender with a capital G is related to the rise of middle class respectability, and in the mid-Victorian period a strong belief in the difference between masculine and feminine traits and behavior was solidified.

Put simply, Victorian gender was a system of social relations and a division of labor in middle class families, in which the man went out into the world to work, while the woman stayed within the home and ministered to the family. This gendered division of labor has become known as "the separate spheres," since men and women were relegated to graphically different places and activities. Within this "domestic ideology," a great emphasis was put on gender difference—the belief that masculine and feminine are different, even opposites of one another. The key idea supporting Victorian ideas of gender was that these roles were based in nature, not culture. Women were thought by nature to be less intellectual, weaker, less able to work than men.

John Ruskin's essay "Of Queen's Gardens" (1865, Nord) is often taken as a comprehensive expression of the Victorian ideals of masculine and feminine virtues, duties, and characters.

> Now their separate characters are briefly these. The man's power is active, progressive, defensive. He is eminently the doer, the creator, the discoverer, the defender. His intellect is for speculation and invention; his energy for adventure, for war, and for conquest. . . . But the woman's power is for rule, not battle—and her intellect is not for invention or

> creation, but for sweet ordering, arrangement, and decision . . . By her office, and place, she is protected from all danger and temptation. The man, in his rough work in the open world, must encounter peril and trial . . . often he must be wounded . . . and always hardened. But he guards the woman from all this.

The "true nature of home," Ruskin writes, is a "shelter" from the outside world.

Not only that, but the middle class, domestic woman is the quintessence of home: "wherever a true wife comes, this home is always round her." This is "woman's true place and power." Upon this domestic ideology the whole world seemed to depend, and the stakes were high (Langland, 1995). As Ruskin put it, to fulfill her ideal role, woman must be "incapable of error . . . enduringly, incorruptibly good; instinctively, infallibly wise." She was the center of the Victorian home, and the home was the bedrock of the nation and even of the British Empire. Woman's presence as its tutelary genius was thought to provide the basis for a protected, almost spiritual arena of goodness, nurture, and innocence in the home. She was the "angel in the house," as Coventry Patmore called his vision of domestic purity, in a long poem by that name (1854–1862).

This Victorian idealization of women depends on their remaining innocent—and even ignorant—of the "dirty" side of life (money, work, or sex). In order that they might one day marry well and become "angels in the house," middle class Victorian girls were brought up to these domestic virtues. It was thought that silence on the topic of sex was especially important to their remaining innocent, and so in this respect innocence became synonymous with ignorance. Today, when we say the word "Victorian," it is usually this prudery to which we refer. And even though our notion of Victorian prudery is probably exaggerated, there is a truth to the stereotype as well. Famous euphemisms (saying "limb," but not "leg") were the echo of social practice (it was not good manners to expose the leg or ankle). Again, these roles and norms are artifacts of the rising middle class (Davidoff and Hall, 1987). From this middle class point of view, working women were regarded with suspicion; their life outside the home was taken to suggest bad morals, and they were often taken to be sexually available. Since there were so few professions open to women, many were driven into prostitution. And women (of any class) who were sexually active outside of marriage were deemed to be "fallen" women, and they were outcasts, quite beyond the pale (Michie, 1993). Meanwhile, middle class women were kept within the home, like children, pets or property. Thus, Victorian wives often seemed childlike in their socialized innocence.

Scholars and theorists in our own time have offered various ways of understanding the relation between sex and gender. One simple way to think about this is to think of sex as biological and gender as cultural. We are born with a sex, but we learn to perform the roles and scripts of gender. We are born male or female, but we learn to act masculine or feminine. This is a good working distinction, but it is too simple, since in reality biological sex influences gender performances and gender roles influence the way we live in our sexed bodies (an example of the former would be the way lactation ties women to their infants and makes a protected environment advantageous, while an example of the latter would be the way cultural scripts of femininity or masculinity lead to the members of that culture finding certain things sexy). Some theorists argue that a distinction between sex and gender can be maintained, while others see sex and gender as inseparably linked in a "sex/gender system" (Rubin, 1975; Sedgwick, *Between Men,* 1985). Despite these complexities, however, this is a good working distinction to keep in mind: sex is biological, while gender is cultural.

Gender norms, roles, and expectations are reproduced in many ways. In the Victorian period, the rules of respectable gender behavior were explicitly codified in "conduct books," such as those by

Carolyn Williams, Ph.D.

Sarah Stickney Ellis, who advised the women of England on their proper roles as mothers, daughters, wives, and representatives of their nation. Social institutions—such as schools and churches—played their part in reinforcing the rules. Literature sits in an oblique relation to all this, presuming to represent (or copy) things as they are—but also attempting to suggest what's wrong with things as they are, and even, sometimes, to suggest how things might be, in a better world. Even novels (to mention only one genre) that end conservatively with the usual happy marriages—as if that solved every social problem and promised a perfect future in the "happily ever after"—might often, in their middles, sketch out unusual and rebellious possibilities for life outside the norms.

Sigmund Freud was an arch "Victorian" in his assumptions about sex and gender—and for the most part, he was more interested in sex than in gender. However, his work does show in many places an awareness of the complex relation of sex to gender. In a section called "The Differentiation Between Men and Women" in his *Essays on the Theory of Sexuality* (1905), Freud notes the fact that the concepts of masculine and feminine "are among the most confused that occur in science." He points out that differentiation in common usage reduces, in many cases, to the simplistic opposition of activity and passivity; that there is a biological difference to be taken into account; but that much of the differentiation is purely sociological. In human beings, he writes, "pure masculinity and femininity is not to be found either in a psychological or a biological sense" (Freud, S.E. 1905, 219–20). Freud's view of the essential bisexuality of humans generally is also relevant here.

Elsewhere, Freud was trenchantly critical of Victorian gender arrangements. He pondered these issues throughout his life and work. As early as 1898 in "Sexuality in the Aetiology of the Neuroses" and especially in "'Civilized' Sexual Morality and Modern Nervous Illness" (1907), Freud developed the idea that culturally-induced attitudes to sex are deleterious to health. Later, he expanded on this idea in *Civilization and its Discontents* (1930).

He points out the grave harm to "young girls, who, after all, are systematically brought up to conceal their sexual life" (Freud 1907, 266). But, as he argues, the systematic delay and concealment of sexual feeling and expression does harm to men and women alike. With the "civilized" delay of sexual gratification until marriage, men build high hopes that can never be fulfilled, as long as young women have been kept in ignorance of sexuality. Those young women come to marriage unprepared for their "role" in it. Even after marriage, with no easy birth control, free sexual expression stops almost as soon as it begins. Freud puts ironic quotation marks around the word "civilized" to mark his negative judgment of these moralistic arrangements. He makes the point again and again: this lack of honesty, this culturally-induced habit of concealment where sex is concerned is literally making us sick.

We have been trying to escape the rigidity of Victorian gender norms ever since the Victorian period. An early twentieth-century feminist, Virginia Woolf, argued in *A Room of One's Own* (1929) that we must "kill the Angel in the House" if women are to emerge from the tyranny of the domestic gender roles. Woolf also points out that the enforcement of female chastity benefits the male; that women thus become like property, owned by their husbands; and that women are consigned to a second-class status if it is made difficult for them to earn money and own property themselves. Conventionally feminine women, moreover—the ones who are correctly playing their assigned gender roles—are relegated to the task of mirroring man to himself "at twice his normal size." That is why Woolf recommends money and "a room of one's own," if a woman wants to become a writer, for she must have independence from these conventional patterns of thought and behavior.

Though some periods of history are more relaxed and others more rigid, about conventional gender arrangements, they do show surprising tenacity over time—the tendency to be reproduced rather than changed. Nancy Chodorow has argued, for example, from a point of view that is both psychoanalytic and sociological, that gender norms are reproduced in part because women are still the primary caretakers of children, a situation that engenders a response of frustration and even misogyny in those children (*Reproduction of Mothering,* 1978). However, the basic idea that it is somehow "natural" for women to perform one set of activities, while men perform another set has more and more been falling out of favor in the twentieth and twenty-first centuries, as women increasingly serve in the military and practice in all the professions, while men increasingly engage in the nurturing of children (and even in "housework"). Still, the problem of the seemingly intractable duality of sex and gender persists. In reality things are a lot more complicated than the reduction of human difference to polarities of two. Freud's theories of sexuality grew out of "sexology," the late nineteenth-century investigation into sexuality in which even homosexuality was defined by normative masculinity and femininity. In sexology's model of "inversion," the homosexual male is seen to be feminine, while the homosexual female is seen to be masculine. This model merely reproduces the old norms of gender within the framework of homosexuality. Again, in reality things are a lot more complicated than that. The rise of gay, lesbian, queer and transgender studies has helped us see how heterosexually-based are our ideas of gender, and how important it is to push beyond the boundaries of these conventional binary oppositions. In reality, there are more than two sexes, more than two genders, and more than two sexualities. (Warner, *Trouble with Normal,* 1999; Sedgwick, *Epistemology of the Closet,* 1990).

However, the critique of Victorian gender norms did not wait for the twentieth and twenty-first centuries to begin. A strenuous critique of the separate spheres—and the particular scripts for both men and women offered in those separate spheres—arose even during the time in which they were most in evidence. Certainly by the last quarter of the nineteenth century, the critique was loud and clear. In a lively discourse on "the Woman Question," all sorts of issues having to do with woman's greater independence were debated: education, property ownership, divorce, courtship and marriage, the raising of children (Helsinger, Sheets, and Veeder, 1983). From various angles of vision, journalists, writers and artists worked to "denaturalize" gender—that is, to show that gender is socially constructed, a function of culture, not nature.

W.S. Gilbert participated in this critique along with many other journalists, poets, novelists, and playwrights. Two plays from 1874, *Charity* and *Ought We To Forgive Her?* both question the sexual double standard. In *Engaged* (1877) he makes fun of gender norms, showing both male and female characters to be performing foolishly during courtship. The women of *Engaged* act perfectly docile, obedient, and innocently feminine, while actually being mercenary, strategic, and able to outmaneuver the men. So, too, in the wonderful libretti for the fourteen comic operas he wrote with composer Arthur Sullivan, Gilbert exposes Victorian gender norms in all their systematic absurdity (Williams, 2011). Like Freud, Gilbert showed that "young girls . . . are systematically brought up to conceal their sexual life." He frequently parodied the exaggerated innocence demanded of young Victorian women, but he also lampooned the old-fashioned masculinity of soldiers, sailors, professionals, and aristocrats. In fact, by representing the absurdity of things as they were, Gilbert's works perform their critique.

At this point it might be useful to distinguish between several different kinds of copying—all of them of interest for this volume. There is biological reproduction, whether by sexual means (involving copulation, gestation, and babies) or by cellular division alone (as in stem cells or cloning). Before technological copying, such as mirrors reflecting images; print and Xerox machines copying pages; and, more recently, forms of digital copying, there were scriveners. There is artistic or aesthetic copying, as in representation, whether in painting, sculpture, or fiction, a kind of copying which purports to offer images of things that exist in reality. And then there is cultural reproduction, which has to do with the way social institutions, norms, roles, and relations perpetuate themselves over time, from one generation to the next, as this chapter suggests.

Pygmalion and Galatea (1871), one of Gilbert's best plays, and certainly his most successful, cleverly raises many "daring" issues about gender and sexuality (Joshua). Furthermore—of interest to readers of this volume—it raises them all in relation to the theme of copying. On the biological front, Pygmalion's wife, Cynisca, wants a child, and at least for parts of the play, Galatea is understood as a daughter-figure. On the technological front, Galatea looks in a mirror and innocently admires her own reflection. And, of course, on the aesthetic front, Galatea is a copy in the first place, an artistic copy of Cynisca's visage (and she is devastated to learn that she is "not original"). But crucially, she does not reproduce correct gender norms and roles, and that is one main point of the play's humor.

Galatea is newly-born (she literally was "born . . . yesterday"), so she has not yet been socialized. Therefore, though in an adult body, she does not know how to "act" the part of a proper feminine woman. Thus Gilbert shows, tacitly, that gender is a function of culture, not nature—and that its strictures are constraining. Galatea speaks freely of her sexual desire for Pygmalion. (Of course, in the play, her desire is called "love," but it's very clear that sexual love is meant.) The fact that her outspokenness seems absurd shows the play's critique of the subterfuge and disguise necessary for women to be correctly feminine. Galatea's innocence seems like sexual "boldness," but is instead "the audacity of innocence." The play shows what real innocence and natural behavior might look like—not the artificial innocence of Victorian femininity.

Pygmalion tries to teach Galatea not to speak out: "Hush! Galatea—in thine innocence / Thou sayest things that others would rebuke," he cautions. But Galatea knows no hypocrisy or subterfuge: "Is it possible to say one thing and mean another?" she innocently asks. In many of his works, Gilbert was interested in the idea of compulsive truth-telling. What would happen if characters were freed of their "civilized" roles and compelled somehow to be honest and forthright? The result is often hilarious, an expression of parodic topsy-turvydom, and "right" reason and correct behavior is usually re-established in the end. But meanwhile, in the messy middle, he raises risky questions. As in *Pygmalion and Galatea,* correct behavior cannot be explained—as Pygmalion, exasperated, says to Galatea: "I have no time / To make these matters clear"—but the play shows the utter given-ness of gender roles. They don't make sense, as Galatea's innocent questioning keeps pointing out, but her inability to intuit the absurd rules is taken by the other characters in the play as a refusal. "The girl will drive us mad," says Pygmalion.

An even more profound line of thought in *Pygmalion and Galatea* dwells on the subject of the cultural reproduction of gender in relation to aesthetic representation. "Pygmalion's statues have one head," the head of his wife, Cynisca. Galatea's beauty is copied from hers. Pygmalion's art is compared to divine creation; the artist is like a god creating life, since of course he does "call the senseless marble into life." Cynisca has given her permission, telling him to "reproduce me at your will." When she leaves for the day, she charges Pygmalion to regard Galatea as her "only surrogate," her "proxy" and her "other self." This flirtatious exchange between husband and wife sets the scene for Pygmalion's temptation, for Cynisca urges him to adore his statuesque copy: "Into her quietly attentive ear / Pour all thy treasures of hyperbole," she urges, meaning his hyperbole about how much he loves his wife.

Art is even more beautiful than life—partly because the real Cynisca ages, while her image (Galatea) does not, and partly because the statue's visage is classically calm (with "placid brow"), while the real woman is changeable, emotional, volatile (she "laughs and frowns," and admits to having a temper). Marriage to Pygmalion has been itself a kind of compromise for Cynisca, since she was virginal, "pledged to eternal maidenhood" as a "holy nymph of Artemis." She wed Pygmalion because of sexual attraction. Artemis imposes a curse in letting her acolyte wed: if either of the married pair is unfaithful, the other can call down blindness on the wrongdoer.

This ups the ante on the value of marital fidelity, which, needless to say, was a primary component of Victorian respectability. Pygmalion, infatuated with his creation, exclaims: "I have no words to tell thee of my joy, / O woman-perfect in thy loveliness!" And Galatea replies, puzzled: "What is that word? Am I a woman?" There ensues a critical exchange about the proper roles of man and woman. A man, says Pygmalion, is

> A being strongly framed
> To wait on woman, and protect her from
> All ills that strength and courage can avert;
> To work and toil for her, that she may rest;
> To weep and mourn for her, that she may laugh;
> To fight and die for her, that she might live!

In response to this daunting litany of masculine works and duties, Galatea professes herself glad to be a woman. This little joke is meant to lighten the seriousness of the exchange, which does double duty in the play, for it shows Pygmalion's entanglement in a near-infidelity with his creation, while it describes conventional Victorian gender roles. First embracing Galatea as perfect woman, Pygmalion then pulls back from the brink of forgetting all other women, including his wife, and says that he loves Galatea "as a sculptor loves his work."

Galatea's love for Pygmalion is of a very different sort. When she describes it, we are meant to notice not only that her love is romantic and sexual, but also that it defines the perfect feminine relation to masculine protection. Galatea describes:

> A sense that I am made by thee for thee;
> That I've no will that is not wholly thine;
> That I've no thought, no hope, no enterprise
> That does not own thee as its sovereign;
> That I have life, that I may live for thee,
> That I am thine—that thou and I are one!

Sander notes in the previous chapter that her love unconsciously suggests an earlier symbiotic relationship with a mother figure.

She begins her life in the play unaware of the difference between male and female. Though of course she will not be allowed to have him as her husband, Galatea here describes the feelings of a Victorian woman about conjugal love, defined as total subordination and merger into the "one" life that is in fact her husband's. Man-as-artist resembles a god, while man-as-lover is still, from this perfectly feminine point of view, in the position of sovereign and creator. At various points in the play, Pygmalion occupies a range of potential relations to Galatea: artist-god, lover-husband, and father. She is ambiguously his artistic creation, a substitute for his wife, and a substitute for the daughter he and Cynisca do not have. Gilbert has cleverly written these risqué ambiguities into the play.

As for Victorian gender roles, Gilbert clearly believes in their necessity, while also seeing their absurdity. Like Freud, he is a hinge figure in this sense—an important thinker who, on the one hand, approved and attempted to explain things as they were, yet, on the other hand, could see what was wrong with them.

We commonly say that to idealize woman is to "put her on a pedestal." The male fantasy of this perfect woman is that she is created for him, has no will apart from his, and loves him with her whole being. The play suggests that this sort of fantasy of total devotion is involved in father-daughter incest (as well as the earlier pre-oedipal attachment to a mother imago); but whether or not we pick up on that suggestion, it is clear that Pygmalion's love affair with his idealistic creation makes him forget the real woman who is his wife. The innocent, Victorian child-woman, the supposed ideal—Gilbert seems to argue—is not a realistic wife. Thus, Galatea's separation from and return to her pedestal is an allegory of gender critique. The pedestal represents not only man's idealization of woman, but also Galatea's primary narcissism. Her individuation and development take place against its background, and (like a navel) it reminds her that she came from somewhere: "Ah, yes," she muses, "I recollect, / There was a time when it was part of me." Against this recollection of once being stone, she plays out the drama of language acquisition, which is also the acquisition of culture, including gender. As Sander points out, and as I have argued elsewhere, Gilbert uncannily seems to prefigure some of Freud's ideas, especially the idea of infantile sexuality (Sander, last chapter; Williams, 2011).

In order to atone for the complications she has caused, Galatea puts herself in the place of Cynisca—perhaps making the play even more risqué, even while undoing its daring suggestion of infidelity and even incest. Acting as Cynisca, Galatea must hear Pygmalion say that he never loved her. Leading Cynisca by the hand, Galatea restores her to her place as wife. Blinded as a punishment for his infidelity, Pygmalion now recovers his sight. Then Cynisca pleads for Galatea, in a burst of female solidarity that can be seen as woman-to-woman or mother-to-daughter. At the end of the play, Galatea climbs back onto her pedestal, undoing the complications of the middle. Pygmalion tears the veil away from the pedestal, revealing the fact that she is now "a statue on the pedestal, as in Act I." At its very end, the play no longer flirts with the idea of biological reproduction and erases the sexual suggestiveness of the middle. As this brilliant and prescient play shows, dramatic re-enactment is yet another form of copying—and a potentially therapeutic one, at that.

BIBLIOGRAPHY

Chodorow, N. (1978). *The Reproduction of Mothering: Psycho-analysis and the Sociology of Gender.*

Davidoff, L., and Hall, 1854–1862. (1987). *Family Fortunes: Men and Women of the English Middle Class, 1780–1950.* Chicago: University of Chicago Press.

Denisoff, D. (2001). *Aestheticism and Sexual Parody 1840–1940.* Cambridge: Cambridge University Press.

Ellis, S.S. (1842). *The Daughters of England: Their Position in Society, Character, and Responsibilities.* London: Peter Jackson,

──────── (1843). *The Wives of England: Their Relative Duties, Domestic Influence, and Social Obligations.* London: Fisher.

──────── *The Women of England: Social Duties and Domestic Habits* Philadelphia: E.L. Carey amd A. Hart. 1839.

Freud, S. (1898). "Sexuality in the Aetiology of the Neuroses." *The Standard Edition of the Complete Psychological Works of Sigmund Freud,* ed. James Strachey (London: Hogarth Press and the Institute of Psycho-analysis, 1959. Volume III, pp. 263–285.

──────── (1905). *Essays on the Theory of Sexuality. Standard Edition,* Volume VII, pp. 219–221.

──────── (1908). " 'Civilized' Sexual Morality and Modern Nervous Illness." *Standard Edition,* Volume IX, pp. 179–204.

──────── (1910). "A Special Type of Choice of Object Made by Men." *Standard Edition,* Volume XI, pp. 165–175.

──────── (1930). "Civilization and its Discontents." *Standard Edition,* Volume XXI, pp. 59–145.

Joshua, E. (2001). *Pygmalion and Galatea: The History of a Narrative in English Literature.* Aldershot, Ashgate.

Helsinger, E.K. (1983). Robin Lauterbach Sheets, and William Veeder. *The Woman Question: Society and Literature in Britain and America, 1837–1883.* Three Volumes. Chicago: University of Chicago Press.

Langland, E. (1995). *Nobody's Angels: Middle-Class Women and Domestic Ideology in Victorian Culture.* Ithaca: Cornell University Press.

McKeon, M. (1995). "Historicizing Patriarchy: The Emergence of Gender Difference in England, 1660-1760," *Eighteenth-Century Studies,* vol. 28, no. 3 (Spring, 1995): 295–322.

Michie, E.B. (1993). *Outside the Pale: Cultural Exclusion, Gender Difference, and the Victorian Woman Writer.* Ithaca: Cornell University Press,

Patmore, C. ([1854–1862] 2010). *The Angel in the House.* Whitefish, MT: Kessinger Publishing.

Rosenberg, R. (1982). *Beyond Separate Spheres: Intellectual Roots of Modern Feminism.* New Haven: Yale University Press.

Rubin, G. (1975). "The Traffic in Women: Notes Toward a Political Economy of Sex." In *Toward an Anthropology of Women*. Ed. Rayna Reiter. New York: Monthly Review Press, pp. 157–210.

Ruskin, J. [1865 (2002)]. *Sesame and Lilies*. Ed. Deborah Epstein Nord. New Haven: Yale University Press.

Sedgwick, E.K. (1985). *Between Men: English Literature and Male Homosocial Desire*. New York: Columbia University Press.

——— (1990). *Epistemology of the Closet*. Berkeley: University of California Press.

Warner, M. (1999). *The Trouble with Normal: Sex, Politics, and the Ethics of Queer Life*. New York: Free Press.

Williams, C. (2011). *Gilbert and Sullivan: Gender, Genre, Parody*. New York: Columbia University Press.

Woolf, V. (1930). *A Room of One's Own*. London: Hogarth Press.

Chapter Three
Mimetic Musings in Art
Tom L. Freudenheim

The impulse to make something that's just like something else—a double—must be very deeply embedded in the human psyche. Although there are examples of cave paintings on six continents, we can only guess about prehistoric impulses; but it's not a stretch to suggest that creating tangible images (as distinct from imaginings) of things seen has always constituted an important form of replication, perhaps to generate a sense of continuity or immortality. Presumably even prehistoric man had some sense, from observation, of the manner in which animals and humans reproduce themselves—that is, create biological copies. We know little if anything definite about the potential shamanic character of the images we find in caves (usually animals) or on pottery shards (often versions of human figures). But it's likely that at least some early historic images have a kind of independent power, so it's not unreasonable to assume that even prehistoric imagery was a meaningful and purposeful gesture, rather than simply a form of random scribbling, and perhaps also replete with personal or group significance. The so-called *Venus of Willendorf* (ca. 22,000–21,000 B.C.E.)[1] and other "Venus" figures of that era probably had cultic significance, but in any case suggest that image-making in imitation of something else (here the female body) was at work.

If the historicity and actual dating of the Abraham narrative in Genesis is up for debate, it's nevertheless interesting to contemplate that post-Biblical Jewish oral tradition (the *Midrash*) includes stories about Abraham smashing the idols in the home of his father, Terah, who was in the business of making idols.[2] The legend is meant to assert the powerlessness of idols (in contrast to the invisible deity), since obviously they are easily disposed of; but it also indicates their power as a threat, else why get rid of them? Were these idols all alike? Were they differentiated? That's not part of the mythology; nor is there a description of what exactly those idols were meant to do.[3] But it's fair to assume that they had some mimetic qualities to them that would have accounted for their presumed power. The dates for the Biblical Moses are also not verifiable, but that doesn't detract from the influence of the Ten Commandments (*Exodus* 20: 2–17, *Deuteronomy* 5:6–21[4]), at least in western culture. The Second Commandment is far too rich to allow here for a full examination of its impact and interpretations. But it clearly involves a prohibition against the making of images—Hebrew: *pesel*, variously translated as 'idol,' 'sculptured image,' 'carved likeness,' etc., as well as Hebrew: *t'muna*, variously translated as likeness, image, representation, semblance, etc.[5] Unlike some of the other Commandments, the Second one retains almost identical texts in both *Exodus* and *Deuteronomy* versions, perhaps suggestive of its consistent importance over time. In any case, it's clear that by Biblical times, mimesis was a fairly common activity, at least in the Middle East. Otherwise, why would it have been so strictly, and unsuccessfully, prohibited?

Based on what we see in the history of art, certainly in antiquity, it's not unreasonable to assume that idols or representations were often meant to look like one another, perhaps based on some ur-models. Their power would have depended on their being widely recognized, and therefore presumably on widely-recognized repetitive and replicated images. Plato understood this when, in the Allegory of the Cave,[6] he presents us with the dilemma about whether images are as powerful as what's "real"; and he worries that art can be threatening—powerful and even dangerous—and sometimes might have to be censored. For Plato, Art is just an illusion and leads us away from truth, in contradistinction to Forms, which were essences, non-material entities of greater importance.

Plato's concerns might well form the underpinnings for issues in Ovid's Pygmalion myth[7]; whereas the Hebrews' fear that images might compete with their 'One' [usually invisible] Deity, probably doesn't come into play here. It's an ongoing conflict between the power of what can only be imagined and that which is tangible. There's something especially threatening about a man-made statue that its creator ends up worshipping—or in any case finds so alluring as to wish it would come to life. It is a version of idolatry, albeit a less menacing and more romantic one than what the ancient Hebrews feared. Obviously the story of a sculptor in antiquity would be appealing as a subject for art, although surprisingly it's not one of the myths that seems to have captivated a lot of Renaissance artists, who often utilized Greek and Roman subject matter in their works. When it does appear, as in Bronzino's 1530 *Pygmalion and Galatea*,[8] the form of the imagery seems to mock religious painting, with the sculptor in effect worshipping his statue, clearly suggestive of idolatry—less an issue in Christian art, where a vast range of characters take on similar poses worshipping a range of images (e.g., Christ, the Virgin Mary, various saints, etc.). But in Bronzino's version of the Pygmalion myth, and in subsequent painters' versions,[9] the unique beauty of the sculptor's own work is what generates his wish for it to take on flesh and blood qualities.[10] It's as much about admiration for the artist's extraordinary skill as about what that skill has produced. He has created something that is like nothing else—either human or inanimate. It's not here that we need look to understand the enormous power of replicating and replicated images. Those tales of independently powered beings have occurred periodically in literature, and thus also in art.[11]

W.S. Gilbert's 1876 *Pygmalion and Galatea* complicates this mythology and suggests the kind of replication in which the world of the visual arts is especially rich. What's interesting in Gilbert's play is the concept that Pygmalion made multiple sculptural copies of his flesh-and-blood wife, Cynisca, although only one, Galatea, actually comes to life, creating the melodrama, which animates the piece theatrically. There's a rich tradition in which the artist creates an image we might confuse for the "real" thing. The idea was alive and well as early as 5th-Century Greece, as we know from the tale of the two painters, Zeuxis and Parrhasius,[12] competing to create the most realistic painting. While it's unlikely that the land-scapes decorating late Roman villas were confused with actual landscapes, there has obviously long been that urge to fool the eye—hence the notion of *trompe l'oeil* painting, which starts to gain popularity in the Renaissance, as scientifically developed perspective begins to be understood.[13] It's a tradition that contin-ues in our own time.[14]

But Gilbert's game of having his sculptor apparently create multi-ple copies of his wife has an even richer tradition in art since, as has been noted above, there seems to be a natural impulse to copy. This is not the place to present a comprehensive history of copies in art, but it's worth reviewing at least some high points. By the 4th century B.C. famous and popular Greek statues were being copied for an expanding Roman Empire's market. As a result, a number of important Greek works are known to us only through the survival of their later Roman copies.[15] The Byzantine church maintained a tra-dition of icons that essentially replicated existing models.[16] This concept of faithful replication was long considered a virtue—in contrast to the need for "invention" that we often associate with art. Specific images were considered imbued with holy and mystical powers, which might be diluted or ineffective if the image were to be changed or developed (suggesting that Abraham was not necessarily off the mark in worrying about his father's idols). A tradition of replicating totemic images based on some ur-model seems to be common in most cultures. As examples we need only consider Buddhist and Hindu deity figures, African masks, or Northwest Coast totem poles and masks.[17]

But there's a far more common form of replicating, which derives from the need to have more of something—probably not the motive of Gilbert's Pygmalion. (Sander's introduction suggests the possible meanings of multiple copies of his wife.) The history of mechanical printing—taking over from the laborious process of hand copy-ing—is tied to the practicality of increased opportunity for distribu-tion. Block printing was done in ancient China[18] and India, although it was not common in Europe until the 15th century. At that point multiple versions of the same texts—and the same [generally reli-gious] images—could be produced. The complex and rich history of print media in western art is closely allied with the importance of wider accessibility for images, and continues to our own day as new media are developed. Issues of "originality" have ensued, considering the relationship between objects and their commercialization.[19] Gilbert didn't have to worry about this in his dramatic creation—although even his play was subject to various knock-offs, as his use of the Pygmalion theme gained popularity on the stage.[20] Artists since the Renaissance have made prints as original works of art, with each of the multiple images considered an "original." Before the wide application of commercial photo-reproduction and machine printing, artists commonly used prints to distribute popular images.[21]

In modern and contemporary art, further questions about so-called originality have been raised ever since Marcel Duchamp's 1917 assertion that a readymade, industrially manufactured, urinal, displayed upside down, was a work of art. He named it *Fountain*.[22] But of course the intention here, both serious and mischievous, was to raise a question not only about art but also about originality. Andy Warhol, especially in his use of photography and his creation of various "versions" of the same image, further raised the same questions, as have numerous artists whose work is created to be sold in "editions." In the 1960s this became so popular as has its own terminology: "multiples." Warhol's use of repetitive photographic images, probably inspired by the stop-time photography of Eadweard Muybridge's studies in locomotion,[23] may even reunite the concept of repetitive image and icon for our own time.[24]

Such an approach is decidedly different from the various casts a sculptor might make of a bronze, since each of these is finished by hand, and theoretically may have variations, albeit often slight, from going through those processes. In any case, if Ovid's Pygmalion was simply reproducing or replicating something he saw, the myth doesn't suggest that the ancient sculptor was creating multiples or editions of his beloved Galatea; it took W.S. Gilbert to figure out that approach. Not unrelated to this discussion of multiple versions (dare we call them "copies"?) is the matter of "performance art" which is very dependent on the moment but is also available second-hand through various forms of recording. Here is an art form whose essence is its immediacy, but in which that essential quality is diluted by the exigencies of market and exhibition opportunities. The question of originality and multiple copies was especially evident during an exhibition of the work of performance artist Marina Abramovic at New York's Museum of Modern Art.[25] By her own implicit definition the artist is the central element in her work. But although she logged in record hours in the one work she performed (sitting still in a chair, staring at museum visitors who sat individually in chairs across from her), the rest of the exhibition consisted of re-enactments (copies?) by other performers, and video recordings of Abramovic's previous performances. This raised even more issues about originality, copies, and an artist reproducing her own work for the purposes of an exhibition. Further questions might be raised in relation to posthumous copies or versions—official or authorized (i.e., meaning "legal" in relationship to international art laws)—of works by sculptors such as Degas and Rodin; it's their presumed originality that gives them their iconic art status.[26] Control and authenticity issues abound in the art world, and we might wonder whether it matters that a reproduction—or, in the theatre, a revival—is actually authorized or authentic.[27] Judgments on such matters are obviously highly subjective.

Some of the avant-garde artists of the 1960s tried to address these kinds of issues. For example, Frank Stella and Jasper Johns—very different from one another—asserted that their work wasn't "about" anything but rather derives meaning from simply being there and wants to be perceived as what it is, rather than some imagined thing it might represent. One might argue about the credibility of this approach (is it really possible to entirely detach an American flag from any meanings and address it as just an object?), but it's not unrelated to the issue of whether a work of art is unique or one of many that are precisely the same (or even "sort of" the same), and whether that matters, if the "thereness"—the work of art simply as an object in and of itself—is really the issue. If the latter, then why can't anything be accepted simply as the thing itself, rather than being turned into a commodity with all the nuances imposed by the market place? The answer of course is that these "things" have all sorts of powers, not unlike those idols Abraham was destroying: the power of value, of status, of mystique, and perhaps even that uncanny value which we think of as the power of art.

The artist par excellence who embodies these questions in a highly unsubtle, if funky, manner is Jean-Léon Gérôme (1824–1904). A prominent and popular painter, who only started creating sculptures relatively late in his career, Gérôme painted himself as a sculptor with his model,[28] clearly suggesting the relationship between inanimate stone and a human being. That this is not simple conjecture can be seen in Gérôme's earlier painting, *Sculpturae Vitam Insufflat Pictura (Painting Breathes Life into Sculpture)*, 1893.[29] Responding to the popular craze for so-called Tanagra figures, following the 1870 discovery of terracotta funerary figurines in Boeotia (Greece), the artist depicts a woman sculptor (Tanagra) adding polychrome to a series of identical figurines—actually copies of a well-known *Hoop Dancer* figure by Gérôme (ca. 1890). Were it not for the sculptor's gender, we might think this painting had been inspired by Gilbert's drama of almost two decades earlier. As noted above, the obsession with this general theme was very much in the air, but Gérôme milked it in at least two other works, of which the most famous is his *Pygmalion and Galatea,* 1890,[30] where there is no more model, but simply a convergence of marble (bottom half) and flesh (top half), which the artist (here not a self-portrait) embraces.

The complexity of the mimetic impulse seems always to have been with us, although interest in this as an art issue waxes and wanes according to the wide range of intellectual passions that are evident at any given time. The expanded opportunities for developing technologically complex works of art in our own time suggests that a great deal we can't even imagine is likely to emerge, even in the near future. And yet we shouldn't underestimate the technological skill required in earlier ages to create works of terracotta and bronze, the latter especially potent for the reproductive opportunities it provides. Art has long been accustomed to its own kind of "cloning." It's interesting to speculate how the challenge of contemporary science and the beginnings of animal and eventually human cloning, scientifically precise replication might impact our perceptions of art. This is not simply about judgments regarding whether something is actually "the same" as something else. Rather, it's the iconic or totemic value that is likely to color our verdict. Perhaps the answer really lies in our expectations of both art and science, their inherent tensions, and whether the worlds of the humanities and science, as once suggested by C.P. Snow[31] are far apart or ultimately subject to many of the same findings, and thus similar attitudes.

End Notes

1. Naturhistorisches Museum, Vienna.
2. *Midrash Genesis Rabbah* 38:1 and *Midrash Numbers Rabbah* 19:1, 19:33.
3. In the Midrashic tale, the idols are said to have fought with one another, and the largest broke the others with a stick.
4. "You shall make you no carved likeness and no image of what is in the heavens above or what is on the earth below or what is in the waters beneath the earth." Robert Alter, trans., *The Five Books of Moses* (New York, 2004), p. 428.
5. See Francis Brown, S.R. Driver, Charles A. Briggs, *A Hebrew and English Lexicon of the Old Testament* (Oxford, 1957), pp. 568, 820–1.
6. Robin Waterfield, trans. *Plato: Republic* (Oxford, 1993), 514a–520a.
7. A.D. Melville, trans., *Ovid, Metamorphoses,* (Oxford, 1986), Book X.
8. Galleria degli Uffizi, Florence.
9. A more popular subject in the 19th Century, with notable paintings by Jean-Léon Gérôme (1890) and a series by Edward Burne-Jones (1875–78).
10. The antithesis of Robert Browning's "My Last Duchess" (1842) whose special, even worshipful, qualities led the

narrator, her husband, to put her to death. Oscar Wilde's *Picture of Dorian Gray* (1891) has resonances here as well, although it's probably more a Faustian than a *Pygmalion* reference.

11. See the various "Golem" stories, especially associated with Prague's 16th-Century Rabbi Judah Loew ben Bezalel; "Dybbuk" tales, e.g., S. Ansky, *The Dybbuk* (1914); Mary Shelley, *Frankenstein* (1818); Coppélia in both Delibes' ballet and in Offenbach's "Les Contes d'Hoffmann"; George Bernard Shaw's *Pygmalion;* and a wide range of other variants.

12. Pliny the Elder, *Naturalis Historia*; see also Jacob Isager, *Pliny on Art and Society* (Oxford, 2010).

13. Examples of *trompe l'oeil* exist as early as Roman mosaics, and reappear periodically throughout the history of art.

14. *Trompe l'oeil* sculpture has become especially popular, from the mundane images of Duane Hanson to the surreal concepts of Juan Muños and the grotesque works of Ron Mueck.

15. The famous *Laocoön* and *Apollo Belvedere* sculptures (both in the Vatican Museums) are examples of copies from earlier Greek works.

16. Sixth-century icons remain models in Eastern Christianity into modern times.

17. The word "totem" derives from the Ojibwe word *odoodem,* meaning "his kinship group."

18. Probably around 105 A.D. with the invention of paper.

19. Walter Benjamin's 1935 essay, "The Work of Art in the Age of Mechanical Reproduction" has become a seminal text in this field.

20. Gilbert's interest in the potential drama of the Pygmalion myth had been preceded by opera composers Victor Massé (1852) and Franz von Suppé (1865); it was obviously a subject of great appeal at the time.

21. John Trumbull's impressive painting, *Declaration of Independence* (1817), became an iconic image because of its availability in widely distributed engravings by both Asher B. Durand and W.L. Ormsby.

22. Duchamp authorized replicas—originals?—to be made starting in 1950.
23. Most of these were executed between 1883 and 1886 in Philadelphia.
24. Apropos of Warhol's late (1986–87) photos of male nudes, Simon Goldhill writes about "the relation between repetition, the cliché, and idealism in the construction of an image of desire. Repetition is fundamental to Warhol's aesthetics." Regarding the repeated images of Marilyn Monroe's lips in Warhol's 1962 painting, Goldhill suggests that this is "a sardonic comment on the circulation of a commercialized icon within capitalism's cultural system." Simon Goldhill, "The Anatomy of Desire" in *Andy Warhol, Eros and Mortality: The Late Nudes* (London, 2005).
25. *Marina Abramovic: The Artist Is Present*, Museum of Modern Art, New York, March 14–May 31, 2010.
26. Two of the most popular works in museums, Auguste Rodin's *Thinker* (1888) and *The Little Fourteen-year-old Dancer* (1881) by Edgar Degas, are known to us primarily via casts that were never touched by the artist. (An entire research project is devoted to figuring out the issues surrounding the various Rodin versions of *The Thinker*: see www.penseur.org).
27. These issues clearly exist throughout the performing arts, and in the worlds of publishing and film.
28. *The Artist's Model*, 1895, Dahesh Museum of Art.
29. Art Gallery of Ontario
30. Metropolitan Museum of Art. *The End of the Séance* (1886, Frankel Family Trust), is an earlier variant on the theme, while *Self-Portrait Painting The Ball Player* (ca. 1902, Musée Georges.Garret, Vesoul) is a later one, both indicating Gérôme's obsession with this myth.
31. C.P. Snow's Rede Lecture, "The Two Cultures" (1959).

Chapter Four
A Glimpse of Things to Come*
Lee M. Silver

> Slowly, inevitably, human nature will remake
> all of Mother Nature in the image of the
> idealized world that exists within our own
> minds—which is what most people really
> want subconsciously (p. xvi).
>
> *Challenging Nature*

DATELINE BOSTON: JUNE 1, 2010

Sometime in the not-so-distant future [*Editor: written in 1997*], you may visit the maternity ward at a major university hospital to see the newborn child or grandchild of a close friend. The new mother, let's call her Barbara, seems very much at peace with the world, sitting in a chair quietly nursing her baby, Max. Her labor was—in the parlance of her doctor—"uneventful," and she is looking forward to raising her first child. You decide to make pleasant conversation by asking Barbara whether she knew in advance that her baby was going to be a boy. In your mind, it seems like a perfectly reasonable question since doctors have long given prospective parents the option of learning the sex of their child-to-be many months before the predicted date of birth. But Barbara seems taken aback by the question. "Of course I knew that Max would be a boy," she tells you. "My husband Dan and I chose him from the embryos we made. And when I'm ready to go through this again, I'll choose a girl to be my second child. An older son and a younger daughter—a perfect family."

Now, it's your turn to be taken aback. "You made a conscious choice to have a boy rather than a girl?" you ask." Absolutely!" Barbara answers. "And while I was at it, I made sure that Max wouldn't turn out to be fat like my brother Torn or addicted to alcohol like Dan's sister Karen. It's not that I'm personally biased or

---

*This essay, the introduction to Professor Silver's 1997 book *Remaking Eden: How Genetic Engineering and Cloning Will Transform the American Family,* is reprinted with the permission of Harper Collins Publishers. The quote at the top is from his *Challenging Nature,* Ecco/Harper Collins (2006).

anything," Barbara continues defensively. "I just wanted to make sure that Max would have the greatest chance for achieving success. Being overweight or alcoholic would clearly be a handicap."
[*Editor's note: The genetic alteration of human embryos described here has not yet been achieved as of this printing, though Lee Silver has shown in his 1997 book how many other once improbable biological events have already occurred.*]

You look down in wonderment at the little baby boy destined to be moderate in both size and drinking habits.

Max has fallen asleep in Barbara's arms, and she places him gently in his bassinet. He wears a contented smile, which evokes a similar smile from his mother. Barbara feels the urge to stretch her legs and asks whether you'd like to meet some of the new friends she's made during her brief stay at the hospital. You nod, and the two of you walk into the room next door where a thirty-five-year old woman named Cheryl is resting after giving birth to a nine-pound baby girl named Rebecca.

Barbara introduces you to Cheryl as well as a second woman named Madelaine, who stands by the bed holding Cheryl's hand. Little Rebecca is lying under the gaze of both Cheryl and Madelaine. "She really does look like both of her mothers, doesn't she?" Barbara asks you.

Now you're really confused. You glance at Barbara and whisper, "Both mothers?"

Barbara takes you aside to explain. "Yes. You see Cheryl and Madelaine have been living together for eight years. They got married in Hawaii soon after it became legal there, and like most married couples, they wanted to bring a child into the world with a combination of both of their bloodlines. With the reproductive technologies available today, they were able to fulfill their dreams."

You look across the room at the happy little nuclear family—Cheryl, Madelaine, and baby Rebecca—and wonder how the hospital plans to fill out the birth certificate.

DATELINE SEATTLE: MARCH 15, 2050

You are now forty years older and much wiser to the ways of the modern world. Once again, you journey forth to the maternity ward. This time, it's your own granddaughter Melissa who is in labor. Melissa is determined to experience natural childbirth and has refused all offers of anesthetics or painkillers. But she needs something to lift her spirits so that she can continue on through the waves of pain.

"Let me see her pictures again," she implores her husband Curtis as the latest contraction sweeps through her body. Curtis picks the photo album off the table and opens it to face his wife. She looks up at the computer-generated picture of a five-year-old girl with wavy brown hair, hazel eyes, and a round face. Curtis turns the page, and Melissa gazes at an older version of the same child: a smiling sixteen-year-old who is 5 feet, 5 inches tall with a pretty face. Melissa smiles back at the future picture of her yet-to-be-born child and braces for another contraction.

There is something unseen in the picture of their child-to-be that provides even greater comfort to Melissa and Curtis. It is the submicroscopic piece of DNA—an extra gene—that will be present in every cell of her body. This special gene will provide her with lifelong resistance to infection by the virus that causes AIDS, a virus that has evolved to be ever more virulent since its explosion across the landscape of humanity seventy years earlier. After years of research by thousands of scientists, no cure for the awful disease has been found, and the only absolute protection comes from the insertion of a resistance gene into the single-cell embryo within twenty-four hours after conception. Ensconced in its chromosomal home, the AIDS resistance gene will be copied over and over again into every one of the trillions of cells that make up the human body, each of which will have its own personal barrier to infection by the AIDS-causing virus HIV. Melissa and Curtis feel lucky indeed to have the financial wherewithal needed to endow all of their children with this protective agent. Other, less well-off American families cannot afford this luxury.

Outside Melissa's room, Jennifer, another expectant mother, is anxiously pacing the hall. She has just arrived at the hospital and her contractions are still far apart. But, unlike Melissa, Jennifer has no need for a computer printout to show her what her child-to-be will look like as a young girl or teenager. She already has thousands of pictures that show her future daughter's likeness, and they're all real, not virtual. For the fetus inside Jennifer is her identical twin sister—her clone—who will be born thirty-six years after she and Jennifer were both conceived within the same single-cell embryo. As Jennifer's daughter grows up, she will constantly behold a glimpse of the future simply by looking at her mother's photo album and her mother.

DATELINE U.S.A.: MAY 15, 2350

It is now three hundred years later and although you are long since gone, a number of your great-great-great-great-great-great-great-great-great-great-grandchildren are now alive, mostly unbeknownst to one another. The United States of America still exists, but it is a different place from the one familiar to you. The most striking difference is that the extreme polarization of society that began during the 1980s has now reached its logical conclusion, with all people belonging to one of two classes. The people of one class are referred to as *Naturals*, while those in the second class are called the *Gene-enriched* or simply the *GenRich.*

These new classes of society cut across what used to be traditional racial and ethnic lines. In fact, so much mixing has occurred during the last three hundred years that sharp divisions according to race— black versus white versus Asian—no longer exist. Instead, the American populace has finally become the racial melting pot that earlier leaders had long hoped for. The skin color of Americans comes in all shades from African brown to Scandinavian pink, and traditional Asian facial features are present to a greater or lesser extent in a large percentage of Americans as well.

But while racial differences have mostly disappeared, another difference has emerged that is sharp and easily defined. It is the difference between those who are genetically enhanced and those who are not. The GenRich—who account for 10 percent of the American population—all carry synthetic genes. [*Editor: Replicating synthetic DNA was announced in May 2010—cf. Epilogue*] Genes that were created in the laboratory and did not exist within the human species until twenty-first century reproductive geneticists began to put them there. The GenRich are a modern-day hereditary class of genetic aristocrats.

Some of the synthetic genes carried by present-day members of the GenRich class were already carried by their parents. These genes were transmitted to today's GenRich the old-fashioned way, from parent to child through sperm or egg. But other synthetic genes are new to the present generation. These were placed into GenRich embryos through the application of genetic engineering techniques shortly after conception.

The GenRich class is anything but homogeneous. There are many types of GenRich families, and many subtypes within each type. For example, there are GenRich athletes who can trace their descent back to professional sports players from the twenty-first century. One subtype of GenRich athlete is the GenRich football player, and a sub-subtype is the GenRich running back. Embryo selection techniques have been used to make sure that a GenRich running back has received all of the natural genes that made his un-enhanced foundation ancestor excel at the position. But in addition, at each generation beyond the foundation ancestor, sophisticated genetic enhancements have accumulated so that the modern-day GenRich running back can perform in a way not conceivable for any unenhanced Natural. Of course, all professional baseball, football, and basketball players are special GenRich subtypes. After three hundred years of selection and enhancement, these GenRich individuals all have athletic skills that are clearly "nonhuman" in the traditional sense. It would be impossible for any Natural to compete.

Another GenRich type is the GenRich scientist. Many of the synthetic genes carried by the GenRich scientist are the same as those carried by all other members of the GenRich class, including some that enhance a variety of physical and mental attributes, as well as others that provide resistance to all known forms of human disease. But in addition, the present-day GenRich scientist has accumulated a set of particular synthetic genes that work together with his "natural" heritage to produce an enhanced scientific mind. Although the GenRich scientist may appear to be different from the GenRich athlete, both GenRich types have evolved by a similar process. The foundation ancestor for the modern GenRich scientist was a bright twenty-first-century scientist whose children were the first to be selected and enhanced to increase their chances of becoming even brighter scientists who could produce even more brilliant children. There are numerous other GenRich types including GenRich businessmen, GenRich musicians, GenRich artists, and even GenRich intellectual generalists who all evolved in the same way.

Not all present-day GenRich individuals can trace their foundation ancestors back to the twenty-first century, when genetic enhancement was first perfected. During the twenty-second and even the twenty-third centuries, some Natural families garnered the financial wherewithal required to place their children into the GenRich class. But with the passage of time, the genetic distance between Naturals and the GenRich has become greater and greater, and now there is little movement up from the Natural to GenRich class. It seems fair to say that society is on the verge of reaching the final point of complete polarization.

All aspects of the economy, the media, the entertainment industry, and the knowledge industry are controlled by members of the GenRich class. GenRich parents can afford to send their children to private schools rich in the resources required for them to take advantage of their enhanced genetic potential. In contrast, Naturals work as low-paid service providers or as laborers, and their children go to public schools. But twenty-fourth-century public schools have little in common with their predecessors from the twentieth century. Funds for public education have declined steadily since the beginning of the twenty-first century, and now Natural children are only taught the basic skills they need to perform the kinds of tasks they'll encounter in the jobs available to members of their class.

There is still some intermarriage as well as sexual intermingling between a few GenRich individuals and Naturals. But, as one might imagine, GenRich parents put intense pressure on their children not to dilute their expensive genetic endowment in this way. And as time passes, the mixing of the classes will become less and less frequent for reasons of both environment and genetics.

The environmental reason is clear enough: GenRich and Natural children grow up and live in segregated social worlds where there is little chance for contact between them. The genetic reason, however, was unanticipated.

It is obvious to everyone that with each generation of enhancement, the genetic distance separating the GenRich and Naturals is growing larger and larger. But a startling consequence of the expanding genetic distance has just come to light. In a nationwide survey of the few interclass GenRich-Natural couples that could be identified, sociologists have discovered an astounding 90 percent level of infertility. Reproductive geneticists have examined these couples and come to the conclusion that the infertility is caused primarily by an incompatibility between the genetic makeup of each member.

Evolutionary biologists have long observed instances in which otherwise fertile individuals taken from two separate populations prove infertile when mated to each other. And they tell the sociologists and the reproductive geneticists what is going on: the process of species separation between the GenRich and Naturals has already begun. Together, the sociologists, the reproductive geneticists, and the evolutionary biologists are willing to make the following prediction: If the accumulation of genetic knowledge and advances in genetic enhancement technology continue at the present rate, then by the end of the third millennium, the GenRich class and the Natural class will become the GenRich humans and the Natural humans—entirely separate species with no ability to cross-breed, and with as much romantic interest in each other as a current human would have for a chimpanzee.

DATELINE PRINCETON, NJ: THE PRESENT

Are these outrageous scenarios the stuff of science fiction? Did they spring from the minds of Hollywood screenwriters? No. The scenarios described under the first two datelines emerge directly from scientific understanding and technologies that are already available today. The scientific framework for the last scenario is based on straightforward extrapolations from our current knowledge base. Furthermore, if biomedical advances continue to occur at the same rate as they do now, the practices described are likely to be feasible long before we reach my conservatively chosen datelines. Whether they are used or not will come down to politics.

It's time to take stock of the current state of science and technology in the fields of reproduction and genetics and to ask, in the broadest terms possible, what the future may hold. Most people are aware of the impact that reproductive technology has already had in the area of fertility treatment. The first "test tube baby"—Louise Brown—is already eighteen years old [*Editor: thirty-three in 2010*], and the acronym for in vitro fertilization—IVF—is commonly used by laypeople. The cloning of human beings has become a real possibility as well, although many are still confused about what the technology can and cannot do. Advances in genetic research have also been in the limelight, with the almost weekly identification of new genes implicated in diseases like cystic fibrosis and breast cancer, or personality traits like novelty-seeking and anxiety.

What has yet to catch the attention of the public at large, however, is the incredible power that emerges when current technologies in reproductive biology and genetics are brought together in the form of *reprogenetics*. With reprogenetics, parents could gain complete control over their genetic destiny, with the ability to guide and enhance the characteristics of their children, and their children's children as well. But even as reprogenetics makes dreams come true, like all of the most powerful technologies invented by humankind, it may also generate nightmares of a kind not previously imagined.

Of course, just because a technology becomes feasible does not mean that it will be used. Or does it? Society, acting through government intervention, could outlaw any one or all of the reprogenetic practices that I have described. Isn't the *non*use of nuclear weapons for the purpose of mass destruction over the last half century an example of how governments can control technology?

There are two big differences between the use of nuclear technology and reprogenetic technology. These differences lie in the resources and money needed to practice each. The most crucial resources required to build a nuclear weapon—large reactors and enriched sources of uranium or plutonium—are tightly controlled by the government itself. The resources required to practice reprogenetics—precision medical tools, small laboratory equipment, and simple chemicals—are all available for sale, without restriction, to anyone with the money to pay for them. The cost of developing a nuclear weapon is billions of dollars. In contrast, a reprogenetics clinic could easily be run on the scale of a small business anywhere in the world. Thus, even if restrictions on the use of reprogenetics are imposed in one country or another, those intent on delivering and receiving these services will not be restrained. But on what grounds can we argue that they should be restrained?

In response to this question, many people point to the chilling novel *Brave New World* written by Aldous Huxley in 1931. It is the story of a future worldwide political state that exerts complete control over human reproduction and human nature as well. In this brave new world, the state uses fetal hatcheries to breed each child into a predetermined intellectual class that ranges from alpha at the top to epsilon at the bottom. Individual members of each class are predestined to fit into specific roles in a soulless utopia where marriage and parenthood are prevented and promiscuous sexual activity is strongly encouraged, where universal immunity to diseases has been achieved, and where an all-enveloping state propaganda machine and mood-altering drugs make all content with their positions in life.

While Huxley guessed right about the power we would gain over the process of reproduction, I think he was dead wrong when it came to predicting who would use the power and for what purposes. What Huxley failed to understand, or refused to accept, was the driving force behind babymaking. *It is individuals and couples who want to reproduce themselves in their own images. It is individuals and couples who want their children to be happy and successful.* [*Editor's italics*] And it is individuals and couples—like Barbara and Dan and Cheryl and Madelaine and Melissa and Curtis and Jennifer, *not governments*—who will seize control of these new technologies. They will use some to reach otherwise unattainable reproductive goals and others to help their children achieve health, happiness, and success. And it is in pursuit of this last goal that the combined actions of many individuals, operating over many generations, could perhaps give rise to a polarized humanity more horrific than Huxley's imagined Brave New World.

There are those who will argue that parents don't have the right to control the characteristics of their children-to-be in the way I describe. But American society, in particular, accepts the rights of parents to control every other aspect of their children's lives from the time they are born until they reach adulthood. If one accepts the parental prerogative after birth, it is hard to argue against it before birth, if no harm is caused to the children who emerge.

Many think that it is inherently unfair for some people to have access to technologies that can provide advantages while others, less well-off, are forced to depend on chance alone. I would agree. It is inherently unfair. But once again, American society adheres to the principle that personal liberty and personal fortune are the primary determinants of what individuals are allowed and able to do. Anyone who accepts the right of affluent parents to provide their children with an expensive private school education cannot use "unfairness" as a reason for rejecting the use of reprogenetic technologies.

Indeed, in a society that values individual freedom above all else, it is hard to find any legitimate basis for restricting the use of reprogenetics. And therein lies the dilemma. For while each individual use of the technology can be viewed in the light of personal reproductive choice—with no ability to change society at large—together they could have dramatic, unintended, long-term consequences.

As the technologies of reproduction and genetics have become ever more powerful over the last decade, most practicing scientists and physicians have been loathe to speculate about where it may all lead. One reason for reluctance is the fear of getting it wrong. It really is impossible to predict with certainty which future technological advances will proceed on time and which will encounter unexpected roadblocks. This means that like Huxley's vision of a fetal hatchery, some of the ideas proposed here may ultimately be technically impossible or exceedingly difficult to implement. On the other hand, there are sure to be technological breakthroughs that no one can imagine now, just as Huxley was unable to imagine genetic engineering, or cloning from adult cells, in 1931.

There is a second reason why fertility specialists, in particular, are reluctant to speculate about the kinds of future scenarios that I describe here. It's called politics. In a climate where abortion clinics are on the alert for terrorist attacks. and where the religious right rails against any interference with the "natural process" of conception, IVF providers see no reason to call attention to themselves through descriptions of reproductive and genetic manipulations that are sure to provoke outrage.

The British journal *Nature* is one of the two most important science journals in the world (the other being the American journal *Science*). It is published weekly and is read by all types of scientists from biologists to physicists to medical researchers. No one would ever consider it to be radical or sensationalist in any way. On March 7, 1996, *Nature* published an article that described a method for cloning unlimited numbers of sheep from a single fertilized egg, with further implications for improving methods of genetic engineering. It took another week before the ramifications of this isolated breakthrough sank in for the editors. On March 14, 1996, they wrote an impassioned editorial saying in part: "That the growing power of molecular genetics confronts us with future prospects of being able to *change the nature of our species* [*Editor's italics*] is a fact that seldom appears to be addressed in depth. Scientific knowledge may not yet permit detailed understanding, but the possibilities are clear enough. This gives rise to issues that in the end will have to be related to people within the social and ethical environments in which they live. . . And the agenda is set by mankind as a whole, not by the subset involved in the science."

They are right that the agenda will not be set by 'scientists, who wield little power in a free society, despite their sense of self-importance. But it's utterly naive to think 'that "mankind as a whole"—unable to reach consensus on so many other societal issues—will have any effect whatsoever. Instead, in the near future, power will lie in the marketplace, and the agenda is sure to be set by individuals and couples who will act on behalf of themselves and their children.

In the pages that follow [*Editor: referring to Lee Silver's book* Remaking Eden], I will explain how remarkable advances in science and technology force us to reconsider long-held notions of parenthood, childhood, and the meaning of life itself. I will show you how technological advances, in particular, provide individuals and couples of all kinds with options for reproducing in ways that were previously unimaginable. And I will present imagined futures—alternatively nightmarish and dreamy—in which people use reprogenetics to assume control over the destiny of humankind.

Throughout, I will explore the ethical arguments that have been raised against the use of this technology. In most instances, I will attribute opposition to conscious or subconscious fears of treading in "God's domain." Indeed, I will argue that nearly all of the objections raised by bioethicists and others ring hollow with one exception not often considered. The power of reprogenetics is so great that if left to the market, those families and groups *not* able to afford it could become severely disadvantaged.

Will a global marketplace based on individual freedom and competition among people and countries reign supreme in the centuries and millennia to come? If so, a severed humanity may very well be its ultimate legacy.

But what is the alternative? So long as sovereign states prevail, international borders can do nothing to halt the passage of cells and genes carried deep within a woman's body. Only a single world state could control the use of reprogenetics, providing it in measured amounts to all its citizens. From our vantage point at the beginning of the third millennium, such a Huxleyan world seems much more securely in the realm of fiction than even the most fantastical scenarios imagined in this book. Nevertheless, the future of humankind is a thousand times longer than its past [*Editor's Note: That seems unlikely as it would be 20+ million years*] and impossible to foresee.

Of one thing, I have no doubt. The growing use of reprogenetics is inevitable. For better *and* worse, *a new age* is upon us—an age in which we as humans will gain the ability *to change the nature of our species.*

Chapter Five
Too Much*
Bill McKibben

For the first few miles of the marathon, I was still fresh enough to look around, to pay attention. I remember mostly the muffled thump of several thousand pairs of expensive sneakers padding the Ottawa pavement—an elemental sound, like surf, or wind. But, as the race wore on, the herd stretched into a dozen flocks and then into a long string of solitary runners. Pretty soon each of us was off in a singular race, pitting one body against one will. By the halfway point, when all the adrenaline had worn off, the only sound left was my breath rattling in my chest. I was deep in my own private universe, completely absorbed in my own drama.

Now, this run was entirely inconsequential. For months I'd trained with the arbitrary goal of 3 hours and 20 minutes in my mind. Which is not a fast time; it's an hour and a quarter off the world record. But it would let a forty-one-year-old into the Boston Marathon. And given how fast I'd gone in training, I knew it lay at the outer edge of the possible. So it was a worthwhile target, a number to live with through one early-morning run after another, a number to multiply and divide against the readouts on the treadmill display when downpours kept me in the gym. It's rare enough in my life to have a goal so concrete and unambiguous.

By about, say, mile 23, two things were becoming clear. One, my training had worked: I'd reeled off one 7:30 mile after another. Two, my training wouldn't get me to the finish by itself. My legs were starting to slow and wobble, my knees and calves were hard pressed to lift and push at the same pace as an hour earlier. I could feel my goal slipping away, my pace dropping. With every hundred yards the race became less a physical test and more a mental one, game spirit trying to rally sagging flesh before sagging flesh could sap game spirit and convince it the time had come to walk. Someone stronger passed me, and I slipped onto her heels for a few

*This essay, the first chapter in Bill McKibben's *Enough* (2003) is reprinted with the permission of Times Books / Henry Holt and Company.

hundred crucial yards, picking up the pace. The finish line swam into my squinted view, and I stagger-sprinted across. With 14 seconds to spare.

A photographer clicked a picture, as he would of everyone who finished. I was a cipher to him—a grimacing cipher, the 324th person to cross, an unimportant finisher in an unimportant time in an unimportant race. In the picture you can see the crowd at the finish, looking right past me toward the middle distance, waiting for their mom or dad, son or daughter to hove into sight. It mattered not at all what I had done.

But it mattered to me. When it was done, I had a clearer sense of myself, of my power and my frailty. For a period of hours, and especially those last gritty miles, I had been absolutely, utterly *present,* the moments desperately, magnificently clarified. As meaningless as it was to the world, that's how meaning*ful* it was to me. I met parts of myself I'd never been introduced to before, glimpsed more clearly strengths and flaws I'd half suspected. A marathon peels you down toward your core for a little while, gets past the defenses we erect even against ourselves. That's the high that draws you back for the next race, a centering elation shared by people who finished an hour ahead and two hours behind me. And it must echo in some small way what runners must always have felt—the Tarahumara Indians on their impossible week-long runs through the canyons of Mexico, the Masai on their game trails. Few things are more basic than running.

And yet it is entirely possible that we will be among the last generations to feel that power and that frailty. Genetic science may soon offer human beings, among many other things, the power to bless their offspring with a vastly improved engine. For instance, scientists may find ways to dramatically increase the amount of oxygen that blood can carry. When that happens, we will, though not quite as Isaiah envisioned, be able to run and not grow weary.

This is one small item on the long list of "improvements" that the proponents of human genetic engineering envision, and one of the least significant corners of human life they propose to alter. But it serves as a decent template for starting to think about all the changes they have in mind, and indeed the changes that may result from a suite of other new engineering marvels like advanced robotics and nanotechnology. We will soon double back and describe the particulars of these technologies. But first consider sports.

"Attempts to alter the human body are nothing new in sports, of course. It's been more than a century since Charles-Edouard Brown-Sequard, the French physiologist called "the father of steroids," injected himself with an extract derived from the testicles of a guinea pig and a dog.[1] Athletes have been irradiated and surgically implanted with monkey glands; they have weight-trained with special regimens designed to increase mitochondria in muscle cells and have lived in special trailers pressurized to simulate high altitudes.[2] For endurance athletes, the drug of choice has for the last decade been erythropoietin, or EPO, a man-made version of a hormone released by the kidneys that stimulates the production of red blood cells, so that the blood can carry extra oxygen. With EPO, the red blood cells can get so thick that the blood curdles, turns into a syrupy ooze—in the early days of the drug, elite cyclists started dropping dead across their handlebars, their hearts unable to pump the sludge running through their veins.

In 1995, researchers asked two hundred Olympic hopefuls if they'd take a drug that would guarantee them a five-year winning streak and then kill them. Almost half said yes.[3] The Tour de France has been interrupted by police raids time and again; in 2001, Italian officials found what they described as a "mobile hospital" trailing the Giro d'Italia bike race, well stocked with testosterone, human growth hormone, urofillitophin, salbutamol, and a synthetic blood product called HemAssist.[4] The British sports commentator Simon Eassom said recently that the only people likely to be caught for steroid abuse were from Third World countries: everyone else could afford new-generation drugs that didn't yet show up on tests.[5] Some sports, like power lifting, have had to give in and set up "drug-free" or "natural" divisions.[6]

In other words, you could almost say that it makes no difference whether athletes of the future are genetically engineered—that the damage is already done with conventional drugs, the line already crossed. You could almost say that, but not quite. Because, in fact, in the last couple of years the testing has gotten better. The new World Anti-Doping Agency has caught enough offenders to throw a scare into dirty athletes, and some heart into clean ones. Some distance athletes who had decided to retire because they felt they couldn't compete have gone back into training; a new group of post-steroids shotputters and discus hurlers have proved their point by winning meets with shorter throws than the records of a decade ago.[7] And both athlete and fan remain able to draw the line in their minds: no one thought Ben Johnson's 1988 dash record meant anything once the Olympic lab found steroids in his system. It was erased from the record books, and he was banned from competition against the odds, sports just manages to stay "real."

But what if, instead of crudely cheating with hypodermics, we began to literally program children before they were born to become great athletes? "Picture this," writes one British journalist. "It is 2016. A young couple are sitting in a doctor's waiting room. They know that what they are about to do is illegal, but they are determined. *They have come to make their child a world-beating athlete,"* *[Editor's italics]* by injecting their embryo with the patented genes of a champion.[8] Muscle size, oxygen uptake, respiration—much of an athlete's inherent capacity derives from her genes. What she makes of it depends on her heart and mind, of course, as well as on the accidents of where she's born, and what kind of diet she gets, and whether the local rulers believe that girls should be out running. And her genes aren't entirely random: perhaps her parents were attracted to each other in the first place because both were athletes, or because they were not. But all those variables fit within our idea of fate. Flipping through the clinic catalogue for athletic genes does not; it's a door into another world.

If it happens—and when that girl grows up to compete—it won't be as if she is "cheating." "What if you're born with something having been done to you?" asks the Olympic dash champion Maurice Greene. "You didn't have anything to do with it."[9] But if that happens, what will be the point of running? "Just what human excellences are we supposed to be celebrating?" asks the medical ethicist Eric Juengst. "Who's got the better biotech sponsor?"

Soon, says Simon Eassom, most sport may become Evel Knievel–ish pageantry: "'Roll up, roll up, let's see somebody who'll break six seconds for the hundred meters.'" Spectacle will survive, and for many fans that may be enough. But the emptiness will be real.

To get a small sense of what it will feel like, consider the 2002 Winter Olympics, in Salt Lake City. While the North American media obsessed over figure skating disputes, the highest drama may have come on the Nordic skiing trails. Erling Jevne of Norway, a grand old man of the sport, was readying himself for one last race, the 50-kilometer, the marathon of winter. He was the sentimental favorite, in part because he had one of those sad stories that, were he an American, would have earned him hours of maudlin airtime. Raking hay on his fifth-generation family farm one day, he'd watched helplessly as his four-year-old son climbed a fence, stumbled onto a road, and was killed by a car. "I don't have a single workout where I don't think about Erich Iver," he said before the Games. "Yes, I would go far enough to say that he is an inner inspiration for my training now"—which makes Jevne not so different from all the thousands of people who run marathons in honor of their mothers, their fathers, their sons, their daughters, their friends who have died before their time or live amidst tragedy.[11] Half the people running next to me in Ottawa seemed to be wearing T-shirts with the image of some dead or dying relative.

Once before Jevne had won Olympic silver, losing to a Finn who, years later, was caught doping. This was his final stand—and he was crushed. Not long after the start, the Spaniard Johann Muehlegg caught up with him and cruised past. "His pace was simply too fast for me. He skied faster than I've ever done in my life," said Jevne.[12] As one commentator put it, Muehlegg "looked like he was skiing on another planet."[13] As indeed he was—the Planet NESP, a new EPO derivative discovered in his urine right after the race. He was stripped of his medal, although he's still appealing.*

Before he heard the news—when he thought he'd simply been passed by a stronger man, or one who'd trained harder—Jevne said, "I'll recover from the disappointment. It's after all just a skiing race."[14] Which is, I suppose, the right way to think about it; for those of us who will never win a race, it should be easy to nod. But as we move into this new world of genetic engineering, we won't simply lose races, we'll lose *racing:* we'll lose the possibility of the test, the challenge, the celebration that athletics represents. Forget elite athletes—they drip one drop of sweat for every thousand that roll off the brows of weekend warriors. It's the average human, once "improved," who will have no more reason for running marathons. Say you've reached Mile 23, and you're feeling strong. Is it because of your hard training and your character, or because the gene pack inside you is pumping out more red blood cells than your body knows what to do with? Will anyone be impressed with your dedication? More to the point, will *you* be impressed with your dedication? Will you know what part of it is you, and what part is your upgrade? Right now we think of our bodies (and our minds) as givens; we think of them as us, and we work to make of them what we can. But if they become *equipment*—if your heart and lungs (and eventually your character) are a product of engineering—then running becomes like driving.

[Editor's follow up: Muehlegg's appeal was dismissed on 16 March, 2002. He was ordered to pay 12,000 Swiss francs to the International Olympic Committee towards the legal costs.]

Driving can be fun, and goodness knows there are people who care passionately about their cars, who will come to blows on the question Ford vs. Chevy. But the skill, the engagement, the meaning reside mostly in those who design the machines. No one goes out and drives in honor of a dying sister.

Sport is the canary in a miner's cage. It's possible the canary will die; there are those who think, with good reason, that genetic engineering of the human organism may be crude and dangerous, especially at first. But the even greater danger is that the canary will be souped up into an ever perkier, ever tougher, ever "better" specimen. Not a canary anymore, but a parrot, or a golden eagle, or some grand thing we can only guess at. A canary so big and strong that it . . . won't be a canary anymore. It will be something else entirely, unable to carry the sweet tune it grew up singing.

No one *needs* to run in the twenty-first century. Running is an outlet for spirit, for finding out who you are, no more mandatory than art or music. It is a voluntary beauty, a grace. And it turns out to be a fragile beauty. Its significance depends on the limitations and wonders of our bodies as we have known them. Why would you sign up for a marathon if it was a test of the alterations some embryologist had made in you, and in a million others? If 3 hours and 20 minutes was your design spec? We'll still be able to run hard; doubtless we'll even hurt. It's not the personal *challenge* that will disappear. It's the *personal.*

The ease with which the power of even something so peripheral can be undercut should give us pause as we move from sport closer to the center of human meaning.

In the spring of 1953, two young academics, James Watson and Francis Crick, published a one-page article in *Nature* entitled "A Structure for Deoxyribose Nucleic Acid." With it they set off the dynamite whose boom is still reverberating. In fact, the echoes grow louder; what was then theory is now becoming practice, first with plants, then with animals, and—oh so close—now with people.

"Genetics" is not some scary bogeyman. Most of the science that stems from our understanding of DNA is, simply put, marvelous—cancer drugs target tumors more effectively because now we understand much about the genetic makeup of tumor cells. But one branch of the science that flows down from the discovery of the double helix raises much harder questions. In fact, it raises the possibility that we will engineer ourselves out of existence.

We unconsciously avoid thinking about genetics too deeply, on the grounds that this science is too complicated for mere laymen, that distinctions between its various branches are surely impossible for normal folk to make. But though you may need years of study to prepare you to *conduct* genetic research, the basic science is easily understandable. And once you understand it, you have every bit as much insight into whether we should proceed with genetic alterations as any Nobel winner. The essential facts are as follows.

Genes reside in the spherical nucleus of each cell of a plant or animal; from that post they instruct the cells to make particular proteins. Those proteins, in turn, key the cell to grow or stop growing, tell it what shape to take, and so on. Grow hair. Make more dopamine. The ways in which we differ, one from another, depend in part on these blueprints, which are inside us from the moment of conception ("nature"), and in part on our experiences in the womb and after birth ("nurture").

Geneticists care about those differences that come from nature—the different pairings of DNA that cue the production of different proteins and hence different people. Some of those differences we classify as genetic disease: an errant instruction from the genes is causing a flood or drought of some protein, and hence a person develops Down syndrome, or cystic fibrosis, or any of a thousand other diseases, most of them rare and many of them devastating. Others of those differences are just *differences:* some people are taller than others, or smarter, and not just because they ate a better diet or read more books. Right up until this decade, the genes that humans carried, in their bodies were exclusively the result of chance—of how the genes of the sperm and the egg, the father and the mother, combined. The only way you could intervene in the process was by choosing who you would mate with—and that was as much wishful thinking as anything else, as generation upon generation of surprised parents have discovered.

But that is changing. We now know two different methods to change human genes. The first, and less controversial, is called somatic gene therapy, and the term is one of precisely two pieces of technical vocabulary you will need to make sense of this discussion. Somatic gene therapy begins with an existing individual—someone with, say, cystic fibrosis. Researchers try to deliver new, modified genes to some of her cells, usually by putting the genes aboard viruses they inject into the patient, hoping that the viruses will infect the cells and thereby transmit the genes. If the therapy works, the proteins causing the cystic fibrosis should diminish, and with them some of the horrible symptoms. No more mucus filling the lungs, no more hopeless cough, no more drowning in your own fluid.

Somatic gene therapy is, in other words, much like medicine. You take an existing patient with an existing condition, and you in essence try to convince her cells to manufacture the medicine she needs. Such a therapy doesn't attempt to change every cell in her body, just the specific type of cells that would be transplanted. The cells of her lung tissue, say. And if she has children, the modified genes aren't passed along; when she dies, they die. Somatic gene therapy could be misused; just as athletes, for instance, misuse medicines to improve performance, so they could inject viruses with genetic materials designed to make their blood carry more oxygen or their muscles grow larger. But, as we shall see later, this is a kind of misuse we know how to deal with, or at least have a frame of reference for. No one I've ever talked to out-and-out opposes somatic gene therapy, and most wish it well. The first trials on a variety of diseases began in 1991; the first real cures were reported in 2001 and 2002; as our understanding of the human genome grows, somatic gene therapy may become more effective. It's not a silver bullet against disease, but it is a bullet nonetheless, one more item of ordnance in the medical arsenal.

"Germline" genetic engineering (and that is the other technical term), on the other hand, is something very novel indeed. "Germ" here refers not to microbes, but to the egg and sperm cells, the "germ" cells of the human being, the basic cells from which we "germinate." Scientists intent on genetic engineering would probably start with a fertilized embryo a week or so old. They would tease apart the cells of that embryo, and then, selecting one, they would add to, delete, or modify some of its genes. They could also insert artificial chromosomes containing predesigned genes. They would then take the cell, place it inside an egg whose nucleus had been removed, and implant the resulting new embryo inside a woman. The embryo would, if all went according to plan, grow into a genetically engineered child. His genes would be pushing out proteins to meet the particular choices made by his parents, and by the companies and clinicians they bought the genes from. Instead of coming solely from the combination of his parents, and thus the combination of their parents, and so on back through time, those genes could come from any other person, or any other plant or animal, or out of the thin blue sky. And once implanted they will pass to his children, and on into time. Does it sound far-fetched? We began doing it with animals (mice) in 1978, and we've managed the trick with most of the obvious mammals, except one. And the only thing holding us back is a thin tissue of ethical guidelines, which some scientists and politicians are working hard to overturn.

You could, theoretically, use this germline technique to prevent genetic disease: you could remove, from the embryonic DNA, the mistake that causes the genes to produce the cystic fibrosis proteins.

But this is unnecessary. As we shall see later, if you've already isolated fertilized embryos, you can simply screen them to see which ones will naturally develop cystic fibrosis, and implant the others instead. No, the reason for performing germline genetic engineering is precisely to "improve" human beings—to modify the genes affecting everything from obesity to intelligence, eye color to gray matter. "Going for perfection," in the words of the DNA pioneer James Watson. "Who wants an ugly baby?"[15] Some of the improvements might sound "medical"—increased resistance to disease, say. But they "treat" illnesses the patient doesn't have, and, as again we shall see later, there's no way to prevent willy-nilly "enhancement" once you've started down this path. The gravitational force that we call civilization is just strong enough to hold somatic gene therapy within its orbit, but germline genetic engineering is power of another order of magnitude—a warp drive, not a nuclear reactor. It will break us free from the bounds of our past and present and send us winging off into parts unknown. That's precisely why it appeals to some.

To make germline engineering work, however, you need one more piece of technology: the ability to clone people. "Cloning" is the one part of this vocabulary that most people already know, and the one thing that scares them. In a way that's a mistake—cloning people is a sideshow, a parlor trick. Who besides rich freaks, and perhaps the grieving parents of dead children, would want exact copies?

The answer is: people who want to do germline genetic engineering. The technique of modifying genes is hard; the success rate is low. If you had more embryos, your odds would improve. That's what the people who cloned Dolly the sheep were aiming for: easy access to more embryos so they could "transform" the animals.[16] Here's how Richard Hayes, the director of the Center for Genetics and Society, and an opponent of genetic engineering, describes it: "It's very difficult to get a desired new gene into a fertilized egg on a single try. To use germline engineering as a routine procedure you'd start by creating a large culture of embryonic cells derived from a fertilized egg, douse these with viruses carrying the desired new gene," and then implant one of the eggs where the modifications worked. "Without embryo cloning, no commercial designer babies."[17] And here's a leading commentator, the Princeton biologist Lee Silver: "Without cloning, genetic engineering is simply science fiction. But with cloning, genetic engineering moves into the realm of reality."[18]

Again, it's not as if cloning is far off, or impossibly difficult. As this book went to press [*Editor: in 2003*], the jury was still out on whether Rael and his fellow UFO cultists had actually accomplished the trick, but in any event several teams of researchers are hard at work. A few flimsy pieces of legislation are all that prevent "reproductive" cloning in most (but not all) Western nations. We've been cloning frogs for four decades; Dolly was the first mammal cloned from an adult cell, but not the last.[19] With humans "it's simply a numbers game," says George Seidel, a cloning expert at Colorado State University. "It's very likely that if you did it enough times you could make it work."[20]

But all this work will require one large change in our current way of doing business. Instead of making babies by making love, we will have to move conception to the laboratory. You need to have the embryo out where you can work on it—to make the necessary copies, try to add or delete genes, and then implant the one that seems likely to turn out best. Gregory Stock, who is a researcher at the University of California and an apostle of the new genetic technologies, says that "the union of egg and sperm from two individuals . . . would be too unpredictable with intercourse. But laboratory conception may not be a burden because such parents will probably want the most up-to-date chromosome enhancements anyway."[21] And once you've got the embryo out on the lab bench, gravity disappears altogether. "Ultimately," says Michael West, the CEO of Advanced Cell Technology, the firm furthest out on the cutting edge of these technologies, "the dream of biologists is to have the sequence of DNA, the programming code of life, and to be able to edit it the way you can a document on a word processor."[22]

All of this is new and unsettling enough that, rather than confront it head-on, people often look for a way out. A common escape hatch, especially for liberals, lies in the politically palatable notion that genes aren't all that important anyhow. We're the products of our environment, so who cares how much cutting and splicing the lab boys do?

Thankfully, there's some truth in that observation. President Bill Clinton marked the completion of the Human Genome Project sequencing by declaring, "Today we are learning the language in which God created life," but in fact creation was written in many alphabets.[23] As Francis Collins, the director of the National Human Genome Research Institute, wrote at the time, "We have seen nothing in recent studies to suggest that nature's role in development is larger, or nurture's smaller, than we previously thought."[24] Not even conditions that seem straightforwardly genetic follow some unvarying Mendelian score; sickle-cell anemia, for instance, which was formerly considered the classic single-gene disease, turns out to come in several strengths and varieties.

In some ways, in fact, the sequencing of the human genome, heralded as the dawn of the genetic age, may really have marked the sunset of a certain kind of genetic innocence. Instead of finding the expected 100,000 genes, the two teams of competing researchers managed to identify just 30,000. This total is still being debated, but whatever the final count, we have barely twice as many genes as the fruit fly, and only slightly more than the mustard weed—which makes it unlikely that genes work quite as simply as the standard models insisted.[25] Indeed, said Craig Venter, who led one of the research efforts, the small number of genes "supports the notion that we are not hard-wired. We now know the notion that one gene leads to one protein, and perhaps one disease, is false. One gene leads to many different protein products that can change dramatically once they are produced."[26] Enterprising academics in fact were quickly calling for research money to catalogue all the new proteins, an even bigger job than the genome work they'd just completed.[27] Meanwhile, those 30,000 genes, though "sequenced," were not understood. Imagine copying the works of Shakespeare by stringing all the words together without spacing or punctuation marks, said the biologist Ruth Hubbard. Then imagine handing that manuscript "to someone who doesn't know English."[28] And the traits that might interest us most—intelligence, aggression—are probably the most complicated and hidden.[29]

Plenty of practical complications make this work harder than editing text on a word processor, too. One researcher told of three hundred attempts to clone monkeys without success—"this process is just so complex," she said, with possibilities for damage right from the moment you harvest the DNA from a cell to begin work.[30] Even if you could perfect the process, simple physics would place some limits on how much you could modify humans. "If you had a nine-foot-tall person," says Stuart Newman, a researcher at New York Medical College, "the bone density would have to increase to such a degree that it might outstrain the body's capability to handle calcium."[31]

All of which sounds comforting: maybe there's not so much to worry about; maybe it's a problem for the grandkids. In fact, however, all these qualifications mask the larger truth: *genes do matter.* A lot. That fact may not fit every ideology, but it does fit the data. Endless studies of twins raised separately make very clear that virtually any trait you can think of is, to some degree, linked to our genes. Intelligence? The most recent estimates show that half or more of the variability in human intelligence comes from heredity. Even the most determined opponents of genetic engineering concede as much: David King, the British editor of *GenEthics News,* writes that "genetic determinism as an ideology is wrong and pernicious, but that doesn't mean that there aren't some completely straightforward, fairly simple, or only slightly complex genetic determinations out there."[32] Richard Hayes says, "My guess is over the next decade we'll find the full spectrum of possible relations between traits and genes: some traits will be strongly influenced by genes, others will have little relation to genes at all, others will be influenced by genes in some environments but not in others. . . . On balance, the techno-eugenic agenda would move forward," unless people stopped it.[33] Stuart Newman, a few moments after explaining why a nine-foot-tall person simply wouldn't work, leaned across his lab bench and added, "But could you engineer higher intelligence? Increased athletic ability? I have no doubt you could make such changes."[34] In other words, this new world can't be wished away. In fact, every time you turn your back it creeps a little closer. Gallops, actually, a technology growing and spreading as fast as the Internet grew and spread. One moment you've sort of heard of it; the next moment it's everywhere.

Consider what happened with plants. A decade ago, university research farms were growing small plots of genetically modified grain and vegetables. Sometimes activists who didn't like what they were doing would come and rip the plants up, one by one. Then, all of a sudden in the mid-1990s, before anyone had paid any real attention, farmers had planted half the corn and soybean fields in America with transgenic seed. Since 1994, farmers in this country have grown 3.5 *trillion* genetically manipulated plants.[35]

Or consider animals. Since they first cloned frogs a generation ago, researchers have learned to make copies of almost everything; it's become so standard that they now need a good gimmick to get any press attention. Texas A&M, for instance, recently called in reporters to show off the first "menagerie" of cloned animals—cows, goats, and pigs. If cloning needed a poster child, it got one in February 2001, when another team of researchers at Texas A&M unveiled Cc:, the first cat clone. The work, funded by a West Coast financier who actually set out to clone his dog, Missy, was not easy; Cc: was the only surviving animal from 87 cloned embryos.[36] On the other hand, according to a university spokesman, "she is as cute as a button."[37] (Soon cat owners everywhere were phoning their neighborhood biologists. One Colorado researcher reported a call from a woman whose cat, Stinky, had died three weeks earlier. She'd stuck his carcass in the freezer and wanted to know what to do now. "I said 'I don't think you've got any hope there,'" the scientist told her. "'Take Stinky out of the freezer and bury him.'"[38])

Under more controlled conditions, however, animal cloning is moving steadily from the lab to the factory—just as with plants, the techniques are increasingly reliable enough to let scientists scale up production. You can order cloned cattle over the Net; a high school student working at a Wisconsin firm managed to clone a cow.[39] Early in 2002, a California company debuted a chip that automates the process of nuclear transfer, the key step in cloning. Whereas now the transfer requires hours of painstaking work under a microscope, "the chip should help make cloning cheap and easy enough for companies to mass-produce identical copies."[40] A North Carolina firm has figured out a similar process for "bulk-growing" chicken embryos, which may soon allow "billions of clones to be produced each year to supply chicken farms with birds that all grow at the same rate, have the same amount of meat, and taste the same."[41]

These same technologies could be used to mass-produce human embryos; "obviously it would make everyone's life easier," said a spokesman for Advanced Cell Technology, the pioneer in human cloning research. But remember: for humans, cloning is a stepping stone. Frank Perdue might be thrilled to see billions of identical chickens, but for his own kids he'd perhaps choose a different nose. Genetic *modification* is the key, and here, too, animals are showing the way. Canadian scientists, to give just one of a thousand examples, have built what they call an Enviropig—three of them, actually, named Jacques, Gordie, and Wayne, after hockey legends. Each of the pigs' cells contains mouse and bacteria DNA, designed to cut down on the amount of phosphorus in their manure and thereby enable pork producers to raise more hogs per acre.[42] Such processes have become so standard that more and more people are getting into the act. In 1999, an artist named Eduardo Kac persuaded a laboratory to rig him up a bunny whose DNA contains genes from a phosphorescent jellyfish. If you hold Alba up to a black light, she glows green from every cell in her body; Kac needed her to "inter-

act with him in a faux living room as a piece of performance art."
Why? "It is a new era, and we need a new kind of art," Kac
explained. "It makes no sense to paint as we painted in caves."[43]

The animal work seems constantly to accelerate. At the turn of the
century, scientists managed to stick jellyfish genes into monkey
embryos—and they tried to warn people to pay attention. "What
stands out," one of the researchers told the *New York Times*, "is just
how simple the method is. If it is refined to be highly effective in
monkeys, it could be just a short step to using it to add genes to
human embryos." Indeed, said another of the researchers, "biotechnology is forging way ahead of biology, ethics, common sense. All
of us think about this all the time. All of the clinicians wonder what
we are doing."[44] But no one—except the venture capitalists pouring
money into biotech—paid much attention. Sure enough, a year
later, in January 2001, researchers at the same lab announced that
they'd managed to produce not just transgenic monkey embryos but
transgenic *monkeys*. A rhesus monkey named ANDi, backward
for "inserted DNA," was "playing normally" with his cagemates
despite the inserted jellyfish genes that made him the planet's first
transgenic primate.[45]

As for the rest of us primates? In 1963, J.B.S. Haldane, one of the
last century's great biologists, said he thought it would be a millennium before the human genome could be manipulated.[46] He appears
to have been off by about 960 years—but then, nearly every guess
about this work has been too conservative. The Princeton biologist
Lee Silver offers a short tour of the folly of underestimation: " 'It is
impossible to determine the sequence of the human genome,' they
said in 1974. 'It is impossible to alter specific genes within the
embryo,' they said in 1984. 'It is impossible to read the genetic
information present in single embryonic cells,' they said in 1985. . . .
All these impossibilities not only became possible but were accomplished while the early naysayers were still alive."[47] As late as
November 1999, *Time* magazine was still talking about the day in
2003 when the human genome would (well ahead of the original

schedule) be sequenced; as it turned out, the work was finished six months after that article appeared.[48] And it's not just the research that's accelerating, but the commercialization: in 1980 it cost a hundred dollars to sequence a single base pair of genes; the price is now counted in pennies.[49] The biotech pioneer Craig Venter said in 2002 that within five years a personalized printout of an individual's genetic code would be cheap enough for anyone to buy, so you'll probably be able to afford it late next week or so. Watch your email in box for special offers.[50]

As we learn more about the human genome, we also get ever better at the mechanics of handling embryos, the technical skill required for cloning and then for germline genetic engineering.

End Notes

1. John M. Hoberman, *Mortal Engines: The Science of Performance and the Dehumanization of Sport* (New York: 1992), p. 72.
2. Ibid., pp. 136, 102; Sharon Begley, "Gold Medal Workouts," *Newsweek,* Dec. 17, 2001.
3. Mark Compton, "Enhancement Genetics: Let the Games Begin," *DNA Dispatch,* July 2001.
4. "More Giro Shocks Still to Come," *ProCycling,* March 5, 2002.
5. Amanda Swift, "The Sports Factor," ABC radio [Australia], July 12, 2001.
6. Ira Berkow, "This Lifter Is Fueled by Natural Power," *New York Times,* Feb. 6, 1994.
7. Rod Osher, "Hot Performances," Time.com, Sept. 6, 1999.
8. Michael Butcher, "Next: The Genetically Modified Athlete," *The Guardian* (England), Dec. 15, 1999.
9. Jere Longman, "Getting the Athletic Edge May Mean Altering Genes," *New York Times,* May 11, 2001.
10. Compton, "Enhancement Genetics."
11. "Erling Jevne: Down to Earth," *Skisport* magazine, translated and archived at www.xcskiworld.com.
12. "Jevne's Last Campaign," *www.langrenn.com,* Feb. 25, 2002.

13. J.D. Downing, "Golden Justice," *www.xcskiworld.com,* Feb. 25, 2002.
14. "Jevne's Last Campaign."
15. Carolyn Abraham, "Gene Pioneer Dreams of Human Perfection," *Toronto Globe and Mail,* Oct. 27, 2002.
16. Evelyne Shuster, "Of Cloned Embryos, Humans and Posthumans," *Yale Law Journal,* Sept. 13, 2001.
17. Richard Hayes, interview, *Wild Duck Review,* Summer 1999, p. 7
18. Lee Silver, *Remaking Eden* (New York: 1999), p. 130.
19. Tim Beardsley, "A Clone in Sheep's Clothing," *Scientific American,* March 1997.
20. Rick Weiss, "Human Cloning's Numbers Game," *Washington Post,* Oct. 10, 2000.
21. Gregory Stock, *Redesigning Humans: Our Inevitable Genetic Future* (New York: 2002), p. 185.
22. "On Living Forever," interview with Michael West, *Ubiquity* magazine, *www.megafoundation.org,* June 2000.
23. "Cracking the Code," *Time,* July 3, 2000.
24. Francis S. Collins, Lowell Weiss, and Kathy Hudson, "Have No Fear, Genes Aren't Everything," *The New Republic,* June 25, 2001.
25. "Nature Beats Nurture," *The Times* (London), Feb. 13, 2001.
26. Tom Bethell, "Road Map to Nowhere," *American Spectator,* April 2001.
27. Richard Lewontin, "After the Genome, What Then?" *New York Review of Books,* July 19, 2001.
28. Keay Davidson, "Sticking a Pin in Genome Mappers' Balloon," *San Francisco Examiner,* July 5, 2000.
29. Francis Fukuyama, *Our Posthuman Future* (New York: 2002), p. 75.
30. Gina Kolata, "In Cloning, Failure Far Exceeds Success," *New York Times,* Dec. 11, 2001.
31. Stuart Newman, interview with author, Dec. 5, 2001.
32. David King, "David King on the Genome Announcement," *Genetic Crossroads Bulletin* 15 (Feb. 21, 2001).

33. Hayes, *Wild Duck Review.*
34. Newman interview.
35. "America's Next Ethical War," *The Economist,* April 14, 2001.
36. "Texas Researchers Clone Cat," BBC.news.com, Feb. 14, 2002.
37. "First Cloned Cat Is Born, Researchers Report," Reuters, Feb. 14, 2002.
38. Gina Kolata, "What's Warm and Fuzzy Forever? With Cloning, Kitty," *New York Times,* Feb. 15, 2002.
39. Brian Alexander, "You 2," *Wired,* Jan. 2001, p. 131.
40. Sylvia Pagan Westphal, "Chip Could Create Mass-Produced Clones," www.newscientist.com, January 30, 2002.
41. "U.S. Firms Seek Mass Cloning of Chickens," Reuters, Aug. 15, 2001.
42. "Genetecists Create 'Enviropig,' " Reuters, June 24, 1999
43. Gareth Cook, "Bunny Causes Outcry," *Los Angeles Times,* Sept. 19, 2000.
44. Gina Kolata, "Scientists Place Jellyfish Genes into Monkeys." New *York Times,* Dec. 23, 1999.
45. "Scientists Genetically Engineer a Monkey," Reuters, Jan. 11, 2001.
46. Daniel Kevles, *In the Name of Eugenics* (New York: 1985).
47. Silver, *Remaking Eden,* p. 245.
48. Sharon Begley, "Designer Babies," *Time,* Nov. 8, 1999.
49. Patrick Mooney, *The ETC Century* (Winnipeg: 2001), pp. 25–26.
50. Susan Watts, "Venter Reveals Clinton Apology over Human Genome," *BioMedNet News,* Feb. 13, 2002.

Chapter Six
The Cloning of Dolly
Jamie Love

I've decided to make **cloning** one of the first topics in this first issue of *Science Explained* because the folks who created Dolly are acquaintances of mine. A few kilometers from my home lives Dolly, the world's first mammalian clone; not counting identical twins. (They're clones too.) What makes Dolly different from identical twins is that she was grown from a cell taken from an ADULT animal! Many bright, well-respected scientists said it couldn't be done. Dr. Ian Wilmut, who is in charge of the lab that created Dolly, admits that he had his doubts. However the hard work and imaginative thinking of his staff made it all possible.

How did they do it and what did they do?

First some background to teach you the basics of *developmental biology*.
An **oocyte** (pronounced "oh-oh-sight") is an unfertilized egg and it has no chance of developing into an animal unless it's fertilized. A recently fertilized egg is called a **zygote** (pronounced "zye-goat"). Funny how the last two letters in the alphabet describe the first stage of an individual animal. For example, a frog zygote normally divides and grows into a complete animal, a tadpole. Later that tadpole will develop into an adult frog.

A cell from a frog's gut should always remain a frog-gut-cell because it has "differentiated." **Differentiation** is the natural process whereby cells specialize into a certain kind of cell. As a frog embryo grows and develops its cells differentiate into nerve cells, blood cells, fat cells and many other different kinds of cells. That's what

Oocyte

fertilization — Sperm

Zygote

cell division

many cell divisions later

differentiation

differentiation is all about. Differentiation is important because without it an animal could never be anything but a blob of unspecialized cells. As a mass of embryo cells divide and differentiate they "create" the animal. This incredible process of differentiation turns zygotes into animals and it's all controlled by the genes. Although the exact process is still poorly understood, scientists agree that differentiation must have something to do with changes in the nucleus of cells. You may recall that the nucleus is the part of the cell containing the genetic material (the DNA all coiled up in organized structures called chromosomes).

What do frog cells have to do with Dolly?

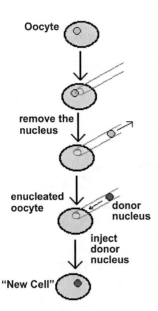

Oocyte

remove the nucleus

enucleated oocyte

donor nucleus

inject donor nucleus

"New Cell"

Like most scientific "breakthroughs" the earlier work done by others provided the foundation on which to try something new. Decades ago a fellow named Gurdon developed the method of "nuclear transfer." This is a two step process.

First he used delicate needles and a good microscope to suck out the nucleus from a frog oocyte, producing an "enucleated oocyte." (That's an oocyte without a nucleus.) With the genetic material removed the enucleated oocyte would not divide or differentiate even when fertilized. That was no surprise. (A cell is nothing without its nucleus.)

But the results from Gurdon's second step shocked a lot of people! He used the same equipment and skill to transfer the nucleus from a frog's gut cell into an enucleated oocyte.

That's **nuclear transfer**, the transfer of a nucleus from one cell to another, creating a "new cell" with a different nucleus. Many of these new cells which Gurdon created behaved like a zygote. They divided and divided and divided just like a normal developing embryo, producing a ball of cells. And this ball of cells differentiated!

Nerve cells, skin cells, blood cells appeared just as they would in a normal embryo. After the normal length of time Gurdon had tadpoles! Because the tadpoles had all come from the gut cells of the same adult, they all had the same genetic material. So they were all clones, identical twins of each other. But unlike normal identical twins they were made from differentiated cells.

Gurdon had proven something that many scientists had argued about. He proved that differentiation was REVERSIBLE. Gurdon's method of nuclear transfer turned back the hands of time, in a developmental sense. Gurdon's method of nuclear transfer made clones from adult cells!

Naturally this got a lot of scientists thinking about cloning. But there were two problems.

First, Gurdon's nuclear transferred tadpoles never grew into frogs! Other folks repeated his experiments and got similar results. Nuclear transfer couldn't clone frogs from frog cells; all you got were tadpoles. No one knew why. Even today, no one knows why the tadpoles made by nuclear transfer die instead of growing into frogs. Weird.

The second problem was that Gurdon's method seemed to work only with frogs (or perhaps I should say "tadpoles"). When scientists tried nuclear transfer with mice, cattle or indeed any mammal, they got nowhere. The "new cells" sometimes divided a few times, but not for long and none of them differentiated properly. You just couldn't clone mammals. By the early 1980's most scientists accepted the idea that something very special allows frogs to be (partially) cloned (into tadpoles). Whatever that process was, it was not found in mammals. The textbooks made it very clear. Differentiation was (sort of) reversible in frogs but not in mammals.

So what exactly did the scientists at the Roslin Institute do?

Well, Keith Campbell, a fellow working for Dr. Wilmut, thought that maybe the cell cycle had something to do with this cloning trouble.

The **cell cycle** is often described as a circle of cell life and division, but I think that can be a bit confusing for some people, so let's try to remember that by "cycle" we mean it happens again and again.

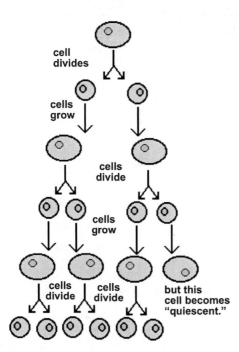

A cell divides into two "daughter cells" and both of these cells live, "eat," grow, copy their genetic material and divide again producing two more daughter cells. Because each daughter cell has a copy of the same genes in its nucleus, daughter cells are "clones" of each other just like identical twins. This "twining" goes on and on with each cell cycle. This is a natural process.

The cell cycle fascinates biologists. Very fast cell cycles occur during development causing a single cell to make many copies of itself as it grows and differentiates into an embryo. Some very fast cell cycles also occur in adult animals. Hair, skin, and gut cells have very fast cell cycles to replace cells that naturally die. And cancer is a disease caused by cells cycling out of control. It's no wonder that biologists think the cell cycle is so important.

But there is a kind of "parking spot" in the cell cycle called "quiescence" (pronounced "kwee-S-ence"). A **quiescent** ("kwee-S-cent") cell has left the cell cycle, it has stopped dividing. Quiescent cells might reenter the cell cycle at some later time, or they might not. It depends on the type of cell. Most nerve cells stay quiescent forever. On the other hand, some quiescent cells may later reenter the cell cycle in order to make more cells. (For example, when a young girl starts to develop breasts.)

Many biologists (including myself) thought that to make a clone you should transfer the nucleus from a fast dividing cell. It made sense because fast cycling cells are exactly what makes an embryo grow. Besides, the gut cells used to make the tadpole clones were fast cycling cells. Many biologists tried to make clones by transferring the nucleus from fast dividing cells but all of those experiments were unsuccessful. (I tried injecting the fast growing cells from chicken feathers into hen eggs in the hope of cloning birds, but it didn't work.)

Keith (Dr. Campbell) thought about it in a different way. He wondered if a quiescent nucleus would be a better donor. True, it was not cycling (that's what makes it quiescent, by definition) but Keith thought maybe that's what the nucleus needs for it to be successfully transferred. Maybe the cell needs time to "rest" before starting to make a whole new animal. Maybe the nucleus needs time, lots of time, to get its DNA in order. Maybe...?

Maybe quiescent cells would work!

So they tried it with cells from sheep.

The folks at the Roslin Institute do a lot of work with sheep as part of their partnership with a company called Pharmaceutical Proteins Limited Therapeutics (PPL Therapeutics). Earlier they had made transgenic sheep (sheep with human genes transferred into them, but that's another story).

They used cells from an adult sheep's mammary (breast) glands for the "donor" nucleus. They grew the cells in **tissue culture**, an artificial situation that is commonly used in laboratories to grow large numbers of cells in bottles. Tissue culture allows scientists to fiddle with the cells and alter their characteristics. That is exactly what Dr. Campbell did. He "starved" the cells of important nutrients and the cells stopped growing and dividing. They became quiescent. (Keith knew they would become quiescent when starved of nutrients because other researchers had proven that years ago; but few folks really cared because who needs quiescent cells?)

And then he made Dolly?

Yes, but creating Dolly was not easy.

Using techniques similar to those used 20 years ago by Gurdon, Bill Ritchie (a technician working with Dr. Campbell) removed the nucleus from an oocyte that was collected from a Scottish Blackface ewe. (Ewes are female sheep. The Scottish Black-face breed is a common breed of sheep in Scotland easily identified by its black face.)

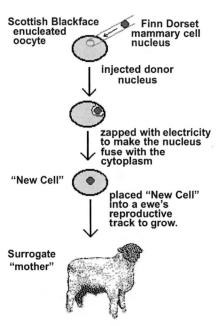

Scottish Blackface enucleated oocyte

Finn Dorset mammary cell nucleus

injected donor nucleus

zapped with electricity to make the nucleus fuse with the cytoplasm

"New Cell"

placed "New Cell" into a ewe's reproductive track to grow.

Surrogate "mother"

Oocytes have a "shell" of proteins and fibers (called the **zona pellucida**) and it is through this protective coat that Bill injected the nucleus from a quiescent mammary cell into the enucleated oocyte. That cell nucleus was from a different breed of sheep called a Finn Dorset, which happens to be a pure white breed of sheep. He then used a tiny pulse of electricity to cause the new nucleus to fuse with the enucleated oocyte's cytoplasm. (**Cytoplasm** is the solution inside the cell.) This electricity also helps "kick start" cells into "activity" so they are more likely to divide. This new, fused cell (containing the Finn Dorset mammary cell nucleus in the cytoplasm of a previously enucleated Blackface oocyte) was transferred into the reproductive "chamber" of a Blackface ewe (the same breed that provided the oocyte).

Bill and his fellow researchers than repeated this process 276 times! That's right, **276 times**.

I told you this wasn't easy.

After 148 days, a normal length of time for the Finn Dorset breed of sheep, Dolly was born (5 July 1996).

As you can see she is a healthy, normal looking Finn Dorset. (Dolly's the wee one on the left) born to a Blackface ewe (her mom's on the right). This proves that Dolly wasn't the product of a sneaky mating; Dolly's Blackface mom could not produce a white faced sheep no matter who was the father. (It has to do with the genetics of sheep breeds.) But just to be sure, the scientists DNA "fingerprinted" Dolly and her "mom" and proved that Dolly's DNA matched the cells from the tissue culture, not the cells from the ewe that gave birth to her.

Dolly is a normal (Finn Dorset) sheep. Contrary to the reports in some of the trash newspapers, she has not eaten her keeper or her fellow sheep. She does not shoot laser beams out of her eyes or talk. Dolly is a friendly, normal, healthy sheep who enjoys being petted, especially if you have some food in your hand!

You may be surprised to learn that clones had been made at the Roslin Institute before, but those clones were made from the nucleus of embryo cells not adult cells.

If you liked learning about Dolly, you might enjoy learning about Genetics. I offer a complete **self-paced** Genetics course specially created for **self-learning**: *"Principles of Genetics,"* on the following website: http://www.synapses.co.uk/genetics/gene.html

Chapter Seven
The Current State of Stem-Cell Research*
Jonathan Shaw

Your mother has had difficulty walking, and this morning she is slurring her words. Concerned that she might have had a stroke, you rush her to the hospital. Doctors there have a different theory: she might have ALS (amyotrophic lateral sclerosis), a disease of the nervous system, specifically of the motor neurons that control the muscles. Without treatment, she would have three to five years to live.

A nurse takes a biopsy to collect some of her skin cells. A laboratory technician quickly cultures some of them in a petri dish, then adds a chemical cocktail that directly reprograms the skin cells, turning them in a single step into motor neurons. These transformed cells, identical to your mother's motor neurons, can now be easily tested for the known defect associated with ALS.

The test confirms the diagnosis. The doctors have a drug that will prevent or slow progression of the disease, but the treatment is toxic to the heart muscle in 20 percent of patients, so more tests are required. During the course of a week, using the same skin cells, physician-scientists use another chemical cocktail to create an induced pluripotent stem cell (iPS) that is capable of producing genetically perfect copies of every cell in your mother's body. Then, applying what science has learned about developmental biology, they use chemical signals to guide the iPS cell, in a series of divisions, to differentiate into cardiomyocytes (cells of the heart)—creating a thin layer of them that actually beats in a petri dish. Now they can test the drug for toxicity against your mother's own heart cells. The cardiomyocytes keep beating, so she can safely take the drug. It is time to go home.

In reality, deriving an iPS cell line takes as long as a year, and there is still no cure for ALS. But this scenario illustrates the tangible

---

*This essay, originally titled "Tools and Tests: The Evolution of Stem-Cell Research," was published in 2010 and is reprinted with the permission of *Harvard Magazine*.

progress scientists have made in using stem cells as *tools:* to change the state of cells; to understand disease mechanisms; and to speed drug discovery. Many of the pathbreaking discoveries in the field—directly reprogramming defective motor neurons caused by ALS, drugs that halt or slow cellular degeneration in the lab, and the beating layer of heart muscle—*are* real, and were made by Harvard scientists. Stem-cell researchers are even beginning to learn how to harness the body's own repair mechanisms to promote healthy aging.

Research on stem cells, once hailed primarily for the promise of cell-transplant therapies, is flourishing in new areas even as progress toward that initial goal continues. "We have not given up on the goal of transplanting cells back and repairing the body," says Cabot professor of the natural sciences Douglas Melton, co-director of the Harvard Stem Cell Institute (HSCI; www.hcsi.harvard.edu), "but this new aspect of using stem cells as tools for drug discovery has got us really excited. And that could lead to the first products, using stem cells as tools to find . . . drugs that slow degeneration."

Two HSCI "core facilities" in particular have turbocharged the pace of discovery. These specialized laboratories—one devoted to creating new disease-specific stem-cell lines, the other to screening chemicals in order to advance human therapies—act as centers of expertise for scientists throughout the University. Each is itself a scientific instrument, as well as a constant source of new tools.

The Ethical Stem Cell
Reprogramming adult cells to become "pluripotent"

Chad Cowan, tall, laid-back, and lean, leads the iPS core facility. The first induced pluripotent stem cell, he explains, was created in 2006 when Shinya Yamanaka of Tokyo University demonstrated that it was possible to reset mouse skin cells to a "pluripotent" state—in which they could become any cell in the body. The advantages of transferring this approach to human beings were clear.

First, the technique raised the possibility that the ethically compli-cated human embryonic stem cells (HESCs) harvested from days-old embryos might no longer be needed. (To date, this has not proven true.) And second, as HSCI scientists immediately recog-nized, the technique also made it possible to create stem-cell lines—an infinite source of cells—from individual patients with specific diseases. (HESCs are not as useful for studying disease, because the embryos from which they come are presumed healthy.)

Having a renewable source of diseased cells in a lab, says Cowan, an assistant professor of medicine, stem-cell and regenerative biol-ogy, "is like having a little human in a dish. You can ask all the same questions about human biology and human disease that you could ask of an actual human patient, only better."

George Daley was among the first scientists to report reprogram-ming *human* iPS cells, Cowan continues. An associate professor of biological chemistry and molecular pharmacology and of pediatrics at Harvard Medical School (HMS), Daley created cell lines repre-senting 10 different kinds of illness, ranging from "bubble-boy" disease to Parkinson's; today, he chairs the steering committee for the iPS core. Meanwhile, his colleague Kevin Eggan, an assistant professor of stem cell and regenerative biology in the Faculty of Arts and Sciences (FAS), derived motor neurons from a patient with ALS. *Science* magazine called the reprogramming of cells the breakthrough of the year for 2008.

Even so, the derivation of pluripotent cells has not been perfected, Cowan explains. To create the first iPS cells from mice, Yamanaka used a combination of four retroviruses that became integrated into the genome of the cell, leaving it slightly different genetically from the original cell. Even worse, the technique involved cancer-causing oncogenes, which meant that anyone hoping to use the discovery in human therapies would need to develop a better approach. A subsequent technique developed by Konrad Hochedlinger, an HMS assistant professor of medicine and of stem-cell and regenerative biology, has eliminated the cancer-causing genes by substituting a different type of virus. "The new technologies are trying to get away from viruses," says Cowan, "because they integrate into the host genome and could interrupt essential or important genes. The iPS core to date is still using a viral-based system, but after you create the iPS cells you can remove it, leaving behind in essence an unmarked genome."

Various labs, Cowan reports, are pushing further, working to replace the genes involved in the stem-cell reprogramming process with "chemical compounds that essentially do the same thing." Eggan, working with HSCI director of translational medicine Lee Rubin, "has shown that it is possible to replace individual genes with chemical compounds," Cowan explains. "Now it is just a matter of finding the right chemicals that work in combination with one another." Daley, who also directs the stem-cell transplantation program at Children's Hospital, adds that "Lots of people within HSCI are working on figuring out more efficient and more effective protocols for reprogramming." Daley himself is developing new ways to make iPS cells from marrow and blood in addition to skin. "Chemicals are one cutting edge," he says. "Identifying pathways"—the sequences in which cells convert one type of signal to another—"that contribute to or stand in the way of reprogramming is another."

For now, the iPS core facility serves two goals. One is to culture, store, and distribute iPS cells already developed by HSCI to researchers worldwide. "We did it as a service for the community," says Daley, "and I think it has been an important one. We have gotten hundreds of requests from labs to receive the lines." (There are currently 14 lines available, with 10 more coming in early 2010.) The second objective is to assist Harvard clinicians and scientists who have unique patients afflicted with diseases they want to study using iPS cells. Generating such customized cells requires "a fair amount of expertise," says Daley, "and the iPS core has it."

"The great ambition, the dream" of the iPS core, says Cowan, would be to "make a stem cell for every patient who walked into a Harvard-affiliated hospital." Daley, whose own work focuses on blood diseases, has a similar vision. The long-term goal of his lab is "to try to couple personalized stem-cell creation with blood regeneration and engraftment": essentially, obviating the need for bone-marrow transplants by using the iPS platform to put healthy blood stem cells back into patients. This approach would eliminate the immune-rejection problems that come with marrow transplants, which often rely on multiple donors.

The challenge is that the patient's own genes would still carry the genetic defect that caused the disease in the first place. But Daley has already demonstrated in mice the efficacy of doing gene repair in a petri dish. One of the advantages of this approach, he says, "is that you could precisely repair gene defects without disrupting other genes," and prove it *before* generating specific cells, such as adult blood stem cells, that could be transplanted into a patient. Such a therapy would be "potentially curative—and safe."

Although such personalized approaches are not yet practical, in part because creating and characterizing a new iPS cell line still takes from six to 12 months, that may not be true three to five years from now. In the meantime, with the technology still in its infancy, one of the steering committee's challenges is prioritizing proposals for making new iPS cell lines. Study projects involving Huntington's and Parkinson's disease and schizophrenia were "among the most mature" proposals initially, says Cowan. Coming soon are new cell lines for polycystic kidney disease and type 1 diabetes.

Having iPS cell lines for various illnesses puts a powerful tool in the hands of researchers who may not know much about stem cells, but who are experts in particular types of disease, he says. For example, iPS cells will allow researchers to compare genetic and nongenetic forms of degenerative conditions, perhaps pointing to common pathways between the two forms of illness. Such pathways could become the target of drug therapies. And iPS cells also allow researchers to watch a given disease unfold. By the time many patients see a doctor, their illnesses are already full-blown, making it next to impossible to determine how they started. The iPS cells will allow researchers to watch, over and over, how diseases progress, so they can test ways to intervene. One day, iPS cells might even enable a full-scale clinical trial in a petri dish.

Cowan's own research on adipocytes (fat cells) illustrates how iPS cells could accelerate research into the causes of obesity. He seeks to learn why, for example, some people can eat everything and remain rail-thin, while others gain weight on a modest diet. If there are genetic predispositions to obesity, clearly they interact with environmental and behavioral factors. Studying cells in a petri dish allows Cowan to control for those nongenetic variables. "You can just say, 'Oh look, *this* fat cell doesn't utilize lipids in the same way this normal fat cell does,' and 'Can we fix that by, say, giving it a chemical compound that will mimic the normal function?'"

Using iPS cells also lets him perform experiments at a scale that wouldn't be possible if he had to rely on human subjects—liposuction patients, for example—for all the cells he needs. "We need to make thousands or even millions of fat cells if we want to screen chemical compounds for their effect on fat," he explains, and iPS cells provide a "reliable, renewable source.

Conditions like obesity and cardiovascular disease also involve multiple cell types signaling to each other: hypothalamic neurons communicating with fat cells in the case of obesity, or liver cells, fat, and vascular endothelial cells in the case of heart disease. To study complex interactions like these, Cowan needs *all* these cell types, all derived from the same iPS cell. Such combinations of human cells could then be studied in vitro or transplanted into mice so their interactions could be studied in a mammal model.

The Road to Treatments
Chemical screening to find new tools, pathways, and drugs

In the quest for new tools like iPS cells, says Douglas Melton, it is important not to lose sight of stem-cell science's long-term goal: making cells to transplant into people. For that, the mammalian embryonic stem (ES) cell is still key, he says, because it is the only one that has not been genetically modified. Thus, even as HSCI works to create a bank of iPS cells for global distribution, it continues to maintain the world's largest bank of ES cells, created at great expense with private money during the years when the second Bush administration suspended federal funding for the study of such lines. After the Obama administration reversed that policy last March, scientists anticipated that the Harvard lines would be approved for use in such research. Only a few of them have been. Harvard continues to maintain separate laboratories for many of its embryonic stem-cell lines—at considerable expense—while the NIH [National Institutes of Health] reviews their eligibility for federal funding.

Beyond the political obstacles, scientists still haven't solved the problem of how to direct the process of differentiation in either ES cells or iPS cells to make specific cell types. Recapitulating the normal development program in a petri dish has proven extemely complicated, Cowan agrees. A protein signal that has a certain effect at one stage of the process—guiding an ES cell to become, for example, one of the embryonic "germ layers" such as endoderm (from which the gut, liver, and pancreas develop)—might have an entirely different effect at a later stage, or in a higher concentration, or within a different environmental niche in the body.

One way Melton has dealt with this problem is to do an end-run around the whole process. Instead of resetting a cell to a pluripotent state and then trying to control the ensuing cascade of cellular divisions to create a particular type of cell, he attempted to change one adult cell type directly into another—in a living animal. In 2008, using three transcription factors (a class of genes known to regulate cell fate during early development), he and postdoctoral fellow Qiao "Joe" Zhou succeeded in transforming a common type of pancreatic cell in mice into insulin-producing beta cells. This was a stunning achievement in what is now called direct reprogramming, the process of determining which genes are turned on and off in the cell. And because Melton derived the cells from a related cell type, only three transcription factors were required.

But to duplicate this feat in humans so that it might one day become useful in treating diabetes, Melton will need to identify a drug, or combination of drugs, that will do the same thing. That is where HSCI's second major scientific instrument—the therapeutic screening center, run by Lee Rubin—comes into play.

In fact, Rubin is directly involved in many of HSCI's most important "translational studies"—moving basic research findings toward implementation in medical practice. Finding chemical means for reprogramming and directed differentiation is just one of his important roles. "He is a linchpin," says Melton, "because without him, HSCI is, in a sense, just a basic-science department." Rubin, Melton notes, is "an extraordinarily accomplished research scientist" who worked for a biotech company but has been brought back to the University to advance HSCI's mission of curing disease. "All of the basic science we do here is going to lead either to our making cells that we can put back into people—and that *indirectly* involves Lee—or we are going to find drugs that block degeneration, or harness the body's own mechanisms of repair by activating stem cells, and that leads *directly* back to Lee," Melton explains. "We need to clone *him*."

Rubin got his start in biotech working on a signaling molecule called "hedgehog," a powerful reagent that scientists discovered caused certain cancers to grow more quickly. Rubin reasoned that seeking a countersignal that would reduce hedgehog signaling might stop or slow cancer, so he set up a screening system to find such an agent. His quest eventually led to the discovery of a promising drug that mimicked the body's own mechanism for inhibiting hedgehog. The drug (now a Genentech property in phase II clinical trials) treats medullablastoma, a childhood brain cancer, and basal-cell carcinoma.

As it turned out, another agent that promotes, rather than inhibits, hedgehog signaling was already widely used by stem-cell scientists as part of a "differentiation cocktail" that could turn ES cells into motor neurons. It occurred to Rubin that he could make billions of motor neurons from ES cells to study disease in vitro, something that had never been done before. While he was still working in industry, a grant from the Spinal Muscular Atrophy Foundation enabled him to begin studying that disease and combine his newfound ability to make huge numbers of motor neurons with his screening system in order to find a therapeutic agent. "When pharmaceutical companies screen, they usually use cells that are easy to grow and easy to make in large numbers," he explains. "Those are never neurons." His research was the first to run a large screen using a neuron with disease characteristics: in other words, the first "disease relevant system" to identify therapeutics.

"In biotech," says Rubin, a lively, fast-talking fellow, "the faster you can do things, the better it is." While most stem-cell scientists remained focused on cell therapies, which can treat a small number of diseases, Rubin hit upon the notion of a real expansion of stem-cell use: to make cells involved in many different diseases. At the time, this involved the cumbersome technique of replacing a human ES cell's nucleus with the nucleus of a cell from a diseased patient. Getting the embryos, the approvals, and the money to do this was not easy. The discovery of iPS "jet propelled" the idea by making the creation of disease-specific stem cells much easier. And it raised a significant possibility: that stem cells might be used to both speed up, and lower the cost of, drug discovery.

Developing a drug, including research and testing in human populations, typically takes five to seven years, and another six months
to two years to secure regulatory approval. In the case of diseases
affecting relatively small numbers of people, the costs can be pro-
hibitive. "Suppose you want to study ALS," Rubin says. You must
test therapeutics for side effects, and "under the old system," he
points out, "to find an effect on a small population, you have to run
a large trial. But if you have a disease like ALS where you don't
have that many patients, you can't do many large trials."

But by using iPS cells, that problem can be tackled from the other
direction—by making iPS cells from hundreds or thousands of ALS
patients over time, and then differentiating those cells to make
motor neurons to identify patients for whom the drug might be
effective, as well as cardiomyocytes and hepatocytes (liver cells),
the two cell types most often involved in side effects from drugs.
That way, potential therapeutics could be tested against a wider
array of cells before anything goes into a person, Rubin says. "This
offers at least the prospect of changing the way drugs are developed, in the sense that you would have better approaches for identifying drugs against particular diseases and for testing their safety.
So that by the time you test it in a person, if all these things align,
the clinical studies are smaller and more likely to be successful."

This big idea—"It is really breathtaking"—might turn out to be
true, Rubin says, though it will take years, and "actually finding
better drugs that work in people," to know.

Rubin's therapeutic screening center allows him to screen more
than 30,000 compounds and controls at a time. One of the ways he
"adds value" to HSCI, as he puts it, is by screening for better drugs.
"One of the things that stands between this big idea and reality,"
however, is differentiating disease-specific iPS cells into particular
cell types so that large-scale screens can be run against them. "We
can make motor neurons, but we can't make beta cells. There aren't
that many cells we *can* currently make right now."

Rubin has therefore begun collaborations with numerous labs around Harvard to run screens for compounds involved in determining what tissue type the cell becomes. The center uses two approaches. The first employs previously identified factors present in normal development. The second proceeds blindly, saying, in effect, "We don't know how to do it, but we can recognize it when it happens." Robotic imaging devices allow center researchers to test, for example, for the presence of proteins known to be associated with various stages of cell differentiation. "Instead of one postdoc in Doug [Melton]'s lab testing a hundred things—whatever number is reasonable for a person to test," Rubin points out, "we could test 30- or 40- or 50,000 variations of different kinds of molecules or combinations of molecules to see if any of them work at all."

Rubin and Eggan just published a paper in which that kind of screening was used to find a drug to replace two of the genes traditionally used to make motor neurons. They might be able to replace all of the genes in the next year or two, Melton says. "Lee's powerful new approach has been working spectacularly well."

In January, Cowan and the iPS core facility will move from a location near Massachusetts General Hospital to the Cambridge campus, right next door to Rubin's therapeutic screening center in the Sherman-Fairchild Biochemistry building on Divinity Avenue. The synergies are obvious—and Cowan and Rubin already collaborate. Harvard is among the very few institutions with both this chemical-screening capability and expertise in induced pluripotent stem cells, says Cowan, "so putting the two together is enormously powerful. And then the last ingredient—what makes this the most delicious cake ever, scientifically—is that we have some of the finest research hospitals on the planet. Their understanding of disease and patient phenotypes informs which stem cells we should make, and once we have them, what we should be doing to search for defects." It is a triumvirate that Cowan believes will "give us the opportunity to make discoveries in human disease" that heretofore weren't possible.

"Everything we thought stem cells would be good for, still is true," says Melton. "Now we just have to get treatments into people."

[*Editor's comment: The search for the fountain of youth continues.*]

A Hidden Youthfulness

What if the stem cells in our bodies live on, even as we age? What if they are just asleep, quiescent, like forgotten sentinels nodding off at remote outposts, waiting for orders? If only scientists could discover how to send them messages, could they be reawakened?

"When you're little and fall off your bike," says Cabot professor of the natural sciences Douglas Melton, "you barely remember it the next day and a week later you don't remember it at all. I ride my bike all the time, and if I fall off now, I remember it for weeks." Bruises last longer when you get older. But is the slowness of repair due to some deficiency that arises with age, that stops normal processes from working well? Or is it due to the absence of some youthful factor?

Amy Wagers, an associate professor of stem-cell and regenerative biology, has begun to answer this most provocative of questions— could we marshal the body's own repair mechanisms to slow the process of aging?—with a simple experiment. Using mice that have been surgically joined so that their bloodstreams become shared, Wagers investigated whether the blood of a young animal might awaken the muscle stem cells in an old one and enhance muscle repair.

When Wagers and colleagues joined a young mouse to an old mouse, muscle damage in the young mouse still healed well, suggesting that the older animal did not introduce a defect. When two old mice were joined, as a control, the muscular repair was, as expected, very slow. "You get lots of inflammatory cells coming in, lots of fibrous tissue deposited," Wagers explains, "and not very much new muscle." But when a young and an old mouse were joined, and a leg of the old mouse was injured, the healing was rapid: new muscle formed almost as well as in a young animal. *Something* from the young mouse—an unknown factor circulating in the blood—was reaching muscle stem cells in the old mouse and turning on the biological machinery of repair.

Wagers (already a recipient of numerous awards, like many of her junior colleagues in the same field at Harvard) has established that whatever the unknown factor is, it is not a cell. Recently she has discovered a "partial pathway," previously undescribed in the blood system, that is involved in the process of repair. "The reason we thought the factor that awakens muscle stem cells might be in the blood," she explains, "is that organ systems decline globally with age, which implies that any signal has to reach many different locations." A good place to look for a universal signal such as that, she reasoned, is in the blood.

In fact, her work has already shown that exposing an old animal to the blood of a young animal restores function to progenitor cells in a variety of tissues, not only in skeletal muscle. She is now collaborating with other Harvard laboratories to study such effects in the pancreas, liver, brain, and heart. "This might be a more broadly applicable mechanism," she says, "an inroad for discovering pathways that can enhance repair activity." In some cases, Wagers thinks, induced repair mechanisms that fail with age might overlap with genetic disorders, so that studying these pathways could advance research on cures for certain diseases. At the very least, she suspects that the "kinds of molecules we discover that enhance endogenous repair activity" could someday play an important role in readying tissues for cell therapy, once that field is mature. Adds Melton, "This has gotten us thinking more about not just fixing the human body when it is broken, but about how to harness the natural activity of stem cells for homeostatic repair to keep us healthy. We're not there yet, but I think that is where we are headed."

Epilogue
(continued on the website)
www.Createdinourownimages.com
Fred M. Sander, M.D.

With W.S. Gilbert's *Pygmalion and Galatea* (1876) as stimulus, this book has explored the many ways we replicate ourselves biologically, psychologically, socially, and culturally, and how we create others in images we have of them. Technological advances are turning science fiction into nonfiction. We are flooded by an explosion of visual images well beyond where Tom Freudenheim's mimetic musings in Chapter Three left off. How many images do we each carry on our Blackberries or iPhones? How do these images define, who we—or the subjects of our pictures—are? Will this explosion of selected and manipulated images change the ways in which we communicate, recall who we once were, and imagine who we may become? In two more generations, will such images become virtual reality? We already edit these pictures in advertising, political campaigns, the news and documentaries. When gene manipulation becomes available will we also edit our genomes?

Just as mass-produced and manipulated images have eclipsed the visual arts, when we thought genes were the foundation of our biological selves, along come EPIGENETICS (continued on the website)!

The fact that the epilogue of this book will continue on a website underscores the rapid technological changes we are in the midst of. It speaks volumes as you, the reader (viewer), are invited to respond to the authors—and to each other—via a blog. These technological changes (social networks) exponentially increase the information to which we have access as well as redefine our relationships to one another.

You may want to begin with the following links which carry forward two areas of focus in the book—biological and cultural evolution:

(1) www.pbs.org/wgbh/nova/body/epigenetics.html

(2) http://opinionator.blogs.nytimes.com/author/susan-blackmore

and then on to Createdinourownimages.com

General References and Links
(Updated periodically online at:
www.Createdinourownimages.com)

NONFICTION:

AAAS Science: Regulating Genes.
http://videolab.sciencemag.org/Featured/97836043001/1
AAAS Science: Definining Epigenetics.
http://videolab.sciencemag.org/Featured/650920373001/1
Bergstein, M. (2010). *Mirrors of Memory: Freud, Photography, and the History of Art.* Ithaca: Cornell University Press.
Beyond genetics (1990)
Epigenetics. www.epigenome.eu/en/
"Biology 2.0" (06/19/10). *The Economist.* A special report on the human genome: www.economist.com/node/16349358?story_id=16349358
Chodorow, N. (1978). *The Reproduction of Mothering: Psychoanalysis and the Sociology of Gender.* Berkeley: University of California Press.
Eames, C. and R Google: "Powers of Ten" From atoms, through DNA, Chicago to the universe: www.powersof10.com/
Furcht, L., Hoffman, Q. (2008). *The Stem Cell Dilemma.* New York: Arcade Publishing.
Genome project: http://en.wikipedia.org/wiki/Human_Genome_Project
Gilman, S.L. (1982). *Seeing the Insane.* University of Nebraska Press. Harvard Stem Cell Institute: www.hsci.harvard.edu
Holland, N. (2010). Literature and the Brain. Gainsville:Psyart Foundation. www.psyartfoundation.org
Huxley, A. (1932). *Brave New World.* New York: Harper and Row.
Huxley, A. (1958). *Brave New World Revisited.* New York: Harper Perennial.
Huxley, A. (1962).*Island.* New York: HarperPerennial.
Joshua, E., (2001). *Pygmalion and Galatea: The history of a narrative in English literature.* Burlington: Ashgate.
Julia, I. (2010). Curator, *The Modern Woman.* Vancouver Art Gallery, Musee D'Orsay.
Keller, E.F. (1992). *Secrets of Life, Essays on Language, Gender and Science, Secrets of Death.* New York: Routledge.
Keller, E.F., (2000). *The Century of the Gene.*Cambridge, MA: Harvard University Press.

Kevles, D.J. (2001). *In the Name of Genetics.* Cambridge, MA: Harvard University Press.

Mendel, G. (1822-1844) Afather@ of genetics: www.mendel-museum.org/

New York Stem Cell Foundation: www.nyscf.org

Gilbert and Sullivan website of Boise State University: www.math.boisestate.edu/gas

University of Utah Genetics Learning Center. http://learn.genetics.utah.edu/

Love, Jamie www.synapses.co.uk/genetics/gene.htm *Principles of Genetics.*

McKibben, B. (2010) *Eaarth: Making a Life on a Tough New Planet.* Canada, Knopf.

[Editor's note: Sometime after writing on the future of biogenetic engineering, Bill McKibben must have felt that attention to global warming was a more immediate concern. If you are interested in pursuing this other controversial topic I would recommend this very readable and guardedly hopeful look at what we are facing and what we must do].

Murray, H.A. (ed.) (1960) *Myth and Mythmaking.* New York: George Braziller.

Newsweek. A special report on the human genome. (June 19, 2010) for info, send e-mail to: jillk@fosterprinting.com

Richerson, P.J., Boyd, R. (2005) *Not by Genes Alone.* Chicago: University of Chicago Press

Robertson, T.R., (2005). *Genetics for Dummies.* Hoboken, N.J.: Wiley Publishing.

[Editor's note: These authors attempt to balance the 21st century biogenetic and 20th- century cultural genetic paradigms arguing that these two driving forces in human development are interactive. Confusing to me is their conflating biological evolution over hundreds of thousands of years of the tortoise pace of gene influences with the hare-like rush of culture since we learned to use, record and transmit culture. This transmission of culture from parent to child, from school to student includes individual psychology. In their hundreds of references there is not one citation of Sigmund Freud. (e.g., *Civilization and its Discontents*).]

Scott, C.T. (2006). *Stem Cell Now.* London: Plume/Penguin.

Silver, L.M., (2006). *Challenging Nature: The Clash Between Biotechnology and Spirituality.* Ecco/HarperCollins: http://128.112.44.57/challenging/index.htm
[Editor's note: You believe you have a soul. Think again. You will rarely read a book that makes as convincing a case for the fictional nature of folklore and religious rituals. You will see how adaptive our genetic capacity to imagine gods was for our evolution. Upon completing this book you will have learned enough for a higher degree in the arts and sciences.]

Sontag, S. (1977). On Photography. New York: Anchor Books Doubleday.

Stoichita, V.I., (2008) *The Pygmalion Effect: From Ovid to Hitchcock.* Chicago: Chicago University Press.

J. Craig Venter Institute. First Self-replicating Synthetic Bacterial Cell and other projects: www.jcvi.org

Williams, C. (2011) *Gilbert and Sullivan: Gender, Genre, Parody.* New York: Columbia University Press.

Zehelein, E.S. (2009). *Science: Dramatic. Science Plays in America and Great Britain, 1990–2007.* Heidelberg: Universitatsverlag.

FICTION and SCIENCE FICTION:

Caudill, M. (1992). *In Our Own Image: Building an Artificial Person.* Oxford: Oxford University Press.

Churchill, C. (2002). *A Number.* London: Nick Hern.

Gonzalez, L. (2010) *Lucy.* New York: Knopf

Ishigura, K. (2005) *Never Let Me Go.* London: Faber and Faber.

Orwell, G. (1948). *1984, a novel.* New York: Signet Classic: New American Library c 1977.

Russel, W. (1981). *Educating Rita.* New York: Samuel French. Film produced in 1983.

Shelley, M. 1977 [1818]) *The Annotated Frankenstein.* Ed. Leonard Woolf. New York: Clarkson N. Potter.

Wilson, K. (2005) *Primal Tears.* Berkeley: Frog, Ltd.

CHILDREN'S LITERATURE and GAMES:

Genetics and DNA Science Kit (Thames and Kosmos, UK):
www.thamesandkosmos.com/products/ge/ge.html

Haddix, M.P. *Double Identity.* Alladin paperback, Simon and Schuster

Haddix, M.P. (1997). *Running Out of Time.* Alladin paperback, Simon and Schuster.

[Editor's note: This book has similarities to Ishigura's *Never Let Me Go.* Both deal with communities separated from the general population.]

This page left blank so readers can fill in their own Additional References and Links:

EDITOR'S ACKNOWLEDGEMENTS

The six-foot long strands of DNA in each of the billions of cells in our bodies, as well as the epigenomic factors in our environments, owe their survival and evolution to those preceding us. Similarly, this book owes much to those preceding it. All of us create and influence each other in the images we have of one another through the use of language. To acknowledge all the influences of the past and present on this or any particular book would require libraries. For this volume, one indispensable library has been the New York Society Library where in 2003 I found the only copy of Gilbert's play in New York City. I have also had the pleasure of using that same comfortable library for my research.

I am most indebted to the contributors to this volume. Tom Freudenheim and Carolyn Williams wrote essays specifically for this book in the midst of busy schedules. Jamie Love, Bill McKibben, Jonathan Shaw, Lee Silver, and their publishers, noted in the texts, gave permission to reprint essays highly relevant to the contents of this unique compilation.

Without Lawrence L. Schwartz, of International Psychoanalytic Books, there would have been no book. Over eight months we, and our personal computers, did the work necessary to hone its complex structure. I am grateful to him for his many skills and his unflagging patience. My conception for the cover was elegantly designed by Kathy Kovacic (www.blackhornstudio.com).

Without certain enzyme products to link genes to proteins, life would be short lived. Larry, as well as a number of editors, provided the chemistry in bringing this book to life. They include Nitza Wilens, Matthew Bach, and, as ever, my wife Joelle. Leon Friedman, Robert Grayson, Ashbel Green, Barbara Leavy, George Mandelbaum, Susan Richmond, Mai-Britt Rosenbaum, Michael Rosenbaum, Morton Schatzman, James Wilk, and Robert Winer gave helpful suggestions, encouragement and advice. I am ever thankful for the support of my sons, Stephen and Jason. Kathy Bennett's eagle's eye, while compiling the index, discovered innumerable typing errors. Kat Kopit also contributed to this effort.

Editor's Acknowledgements

An invitation to deliver a talk on the Pygmalion Myth to the Muriel Gardner Lecture Program on Psychoanalysis and the Humanities at Yale University in 2002 set in motion my preoccupation with this fertile myth. I have attended and presented an early version of my ideas on the Pygmalion-Galatea Process to the Richardson History of Psychiatry Research Seminar in the Weill-Cornell Department of Psychiatry. The on-going collegial discussions in that seminar continue to influence my appreciation of the continuities, discontinuities and surprises history presents to us.

To W.S. Gilbert, who wrote *Pygmalion and Galatea* 140 years ago, we are all indebted. I trust he would be pleased to know that, in addition to the continued popularity of the operettas he wrote with Arthur Sullivan, his personal creation of this play, as so many works of art, comes close to immortality.

Robert Penzer, the liason to the centenary committee of the New York Psychoanalytic Institute and Society, was ever responsive and helpful in giving the book legs each step of the way.

To Feliciano at Copy Quest, who was always at the ready to copy pages, chapters, and early bound versions of this book.

In linking psychoanalysis and family therapy with the new world of genomic research and medicine, I thank Dr. Daylin James and Dr. Shahin Rafii, Chief of the Stem-Cell Research Division, and Dr. Dan Goldschlag of the Assisted Reproductive Center at the Weill-Cornell Medical Center for enlightening me further about the current state of their fields.

To Dr. Arnold D. Richards, who inspired and founded internationalpsychoanalysis.net and IPBooks.net, many of us owe a debt of gratitude. He realized, more than most, that the survival of psychoanalysis depends upon greater communication with the outside world. I hope this volume helps to achieve this.

Responsibility for the final contents of this book rests with myself and the other contributors.

—*Fred M. Sander, M.D.*
November 1, 2010

INDEX

C

Campbell, Keith, 148–50
castration anxiety, as trauma of childhood, 16
cell cycle, 148–51
cellular division, as type of copying, 93
Challenging Nature (Silver), 6
Charity (Gilbert), 93
chastity, effects of women's, 91
childhood, couples repeating conflicts of, 16–17
children, 19
   in *Brave New World,* 120
   choosing gender and other traits of, 111–12, 120–21, 128
   conception of, 136
   Cynisca's desire for, 25–26, 50, 85
   discovery of sexual differences, 15
   genetic enhancement of, 115–16, 134–35
   mirroring parents, 18, 21
   parent's somatic gene therapy not affecting, 133
   psychological traumas of, 15–16
   women as primary caretakers of, 91–92
Children of a Lesser God (Medoff), 19–20
Chodorow, Nancy, 91–92
Chrysos, in *Pygmalion and Galatea*
   Daphne and, 76–79
   as patron of Art, 32–33, 39, 65
   wanting to buy statue of Galatea, 63–69
Civilization and Its Discontents (Freud), 90–91
"Civilized Sexual Morality and Modern Nervous Illness" (Freud), 90–91
class
   polarization in futuristic scenes, 114–17, 120
   relation of gender expectations to, 87, 89
Clinton, Bill, 137
cloning, 114, 122
   of animals, 5, 139–40, 147, 149–51
   in art, 4, 108
   choice of quiescent cells for, 148–50
   commercialization of, 140
   control of reproductive, 136
   definition of, 5
   ease of, 138–40
   genetic modifications *vs.,* 140

Chrysos wanting to buy statue of, 63–69
coming to life, 42–44, 68–70
dream of, 12–14, 53–54
falling in love with creator, 4, 9–10
fear of returning to stone, 53
gender of, 14–15
innocence of, 94
love for Pygmalion, 50–55
modeled on Cynisca, 34, 47–48, 94
narcissism of, 14–15, 97–98
not reproducing gender roles, 94–95
portraying infantile sexuality, 11
pretending to be Cynisca, 80–82, 84, 98
problems all blamed on, 74, 79–80, 83–84
Pygmalion's feelings for, 50–51, 81–83, 97–98
Pygmalion's infidelity with, 71–73
return to stone, 10, 84, 98
rivalry with Cynisca, 14, 48–49
trying to actualize wishes, 12–14, 19
as woman, 44–45, 96
gender
choosing children's, 6, 111
constructed by culture *vs.* nature, 93–94
Galatea as woman, 44–45, 96
in *Pygmalion and Galatea,* 65–66
relation to class, 87, 89
relation to sex, 89, 92
gender differences, 87, 90
gender roles
critiques of, 90, 92, 97
Galatea not reproducing, 94–95
persistence of, 91–92
in *Pygmalion and Galatea,* 14–15, 45, 96
Ruskin on, 87–88
Victorian, 6, 89–90, 97
genes
complexity of interactions of, 137
environment's interaction with, in diseases, 157–58
functions of, 132
implicated in diseases, 119, 132–34
influence of environment *vs.,* 128, 132, 137
influence on personality traits, 138–39

possible improvements in from genetic engineering, 126–27
possible misuse of somatic gene therapy in, 133–34
spectacle in, 129
Stella, Frank, 106
stem-cell research, 4, 161
    goals of, 159, 161–62
    implementing in medical practice, 160
stem cells, 5
    cloning as use of reproduction by, 5
    creation of disease-specific, 161–63
    human embryonic (HE), 155
    induced pluripotent (iPS), 153–58, 161
    lines associated with diseases, 153–54, 156–57
    mammalian embryonic (ES), 159, 161
    reprogramming, 155–56, 159–60
    used in studying diseases, 157–58, 161
    used in treating diseases, 153–54, 156–57, 160, 163–64
    used to study aging, 164
    used to study effects of drugs, 162
steroids, 127–28
Stock, Gregory, 136
"A Structure for Dexoyribose Nucleic Acid" (Watson and Crick),
    131–32
Sullivan, Arthur, 93
symbiotic relationship, with mothers, 97

T
technology, 127. *See also* reproductive technology
    advances in cloning, 139–40
    for genetic engineering, 118
    government control over, 119–20
    rate of change in, 1–2, 6, 139–40
    in reproducing art, 104–5, 107–8
    for reprogenetics, 119–22
    unequal access to, 116–17, 121
therapy
    influence of analyst in, 22–23
    integrating psychoanalysis in couple and family, 16–17
    Pygmalion-Galatea Process in, 22
toilet training, 15
transference, 22
traumas, childhood, 15–16